JOURNEY TO FASHION MERCHANDISING

College Admissions & Profiles

Rachel A. Winston, Ph.D.

ISBN 978-1946432599 (hardback); 978-1946432575 (paperback); 978-1946432582 (e-book)

LCCN: 2022902628

Lizard Publishing® 7700 Irvine Center Drive, Suite 800 Irvine, CA 92618 *www.lizard-publishing.com*

Lizard Publishing creates, designs, produces, and distributes books and resources to provide academic, admissions, and career information. Our mental process is fueled by three tenets:

- Ignite the hunger to learn and the passion to make a difference
- Illuminate the expanse of knowledge by sharing cutting edge thinking
- Innovate to create a world that makes the transition from dreams to reality

We work with academic leaders who transform the educational landscape to publish relevant content and advise students of their educational and professional options, with the aim of developing 21st-century learners and leaders. We also work with students to publish their books and present widely diverse ideas to the college/graduate school-bound community. With headquarters in Irvine, California, Lizard Publishing works virtually with authors to edit, publish, and distribute both hard copy and paperback books.

This book was published in the U.S.A. Lizard Publishing is a premium quality provider of educational reference, career guidance, and motivational publications/merchandise for global learners, educators, and stakeholders in education.

Book design by Michelle Tahan *www.michelletahan.com*

Book formatting by Obinna Chinemerem Ozuo

Book website: *www.collegefashionprograms.com*

LIZARD PUBLISHING

This book is dedicated to the outstanding and dedicated servant-leaders at Leadership Tomorrow whom I have worked with for more than twenty-five years.

ACKNOWLEDGMENTS

There is never enough room to acknowledge every person. Numerous people contributed to my perspective about fashion merchandising. Students, faculty, counselors, and researchers assisted in enhancing my knowledge base or taught me indelible lessons. Over a lifetime of experiences working with students, I am wiser and more worldly.

I gratefully acknowledge Michelle Tahan, Jasmine Jhunjhnuwala, E. Liz Kim, and Jacqueline Xu, as well as my family, friends, colleagues, and professors. It is with profound gratitude that I acknowledge those I have known in the theatre world.

As a faculty member in the UCLA College Counseling Certificate Program, I met many dedicated counselors who spend their life serving and supporting students. Meaningful contributions to the book have been made indirectly by admissions representatives, college counselors, faculty members who took a special interest in this book's success.

I would also like to thank the thousands of students I have taught, counseled, or supported in my nearly four decades of service.

Isaac Newton once said, "If I see so far, it is because I stand on the shoulders of giants."

> *"If I see so far, it is because I stand on the shoulders of giants."*
> *— Isaac Newton*

A few of those giants whose broad shoulders lifted me higher and helped teach invaluable lessons include: Austin Ferrero, Jojo Inouye, Nadia Kuba, Willi Wolf, Katie Bozorgi, Hasti Olia, Siyu Chen, Taylor Devlin, Delaram Didehvar, Chenoa Craver, Nicole Knicker, Andrea Montesinos, Katie Foose, Zixuan Lin, Olivia Moxie, Monette Tarvaran, and Maddie Browning.

Finally, there would be no book on fashion merchandising schools and no career college admissions counseling without the support of Robert Helmer, whose tireless efforts support me every single day.

ABOUT THE AUTHOR

D r. Rachel A. Winston is a tireless student advocate. She has served the educational community as a university professor, college advisor, statistician, researcher, author, cryptanalyst, motivational speaker, publishing executive, and lifelong student. As one of the leading experts in college counseling and an award-winning faculty member, Dr. Winston has spent her lifetime learning, teaching, mentoring, and coaching students. Her counseling practice centers around college admissions, college essays, portfolios, and intellectual conversations about life and career pursuits.

She started college at thirteen and graduated from college programs in such widely ranging disciplines as chemistry, mathematics, computers, liberal arts, international relations, negotiation, conflict resolution, peacebuilding, business administration, higher education leadership, interpreting, college counseling, and publishing. Throughout her education, she attended and graduated from Harvard, University of Chicago, University of Texas, GWU, UCLA, Syracuse, CSUF, CSUDH, Pepperdine, Claremont Graduate University, and Gallaudet University.

Her position working in Washington, D.C. on Capitol Hill and with the White House in the 1980s took her to approximately a hundred universities training campaign managers at colleges from Colorado to California, thoroughly dotting the western states. Later, she led college tours with students and their families on road trips throughout the United States. She has taught or counseled thousands of students over her career and speaks at conferences and academic programs throughout the world.

As a professor and avid writer for numerous publications, she won the 2012 McFarland Literary Achievement Award, Bletchley Park Cryptanalyst Award, and numerous other awards, including Faculty Member of the Year, Leadership Tomorrow Leader of the Year, and college service and leadership awards. While studying Human Capital at Claremont Graduate University, she was a scholarship recipient at the Drucker School of Management. She was also elected to the statewide Board of Governors for the Faculty Association for California Community Colleges, where she served on their executive committee.

She served as a faculty member for the UCLA College Counselor Certificate Program, the Director of Mathematics at Brandman University, and Embry Riddle Aeronautical University, Chapman University, Cal State Fullerton, and a handful of California Community Colleges, including Cerro Coso College where she also served as the Academic Senate President and retired in 2016. Over her career, she taught mathematics online, on television, live interactive satellite, telecourses, and in large and small lecture halls.

AUTHOR'S NOTE

You are reading this book because you are considering admission to colleges where you open the doors to the world of fashion merchandising. Whatever route you took to get to this point, you are in the right place. Right now, you need to gather information to make informed decisions.

While many people offer advice, suggestions differ. Friends will tell you the 'right' way or the way their neighbor was accepted. Graciously accept this anecdotal information while you commit to learning more. This opportunity to pursue fashion merchandising is available so you can pursue your future.

Dig deeper to consider both expert and current information from counselors who have worked with hundreds of students. Changes in programs, curricula, requirements, and links happen each year.

Doublecheck each program's specifics yourself. This guide is current as of January 2022, with each school's profile information. However, since researching this book, changes may have taken place. There are other books about fashion merchandising programs written by talented and experienced counselors. We admire and cheer on their efforts.

"We are what we think. All that we are arises with our thoughts. With our thoughts, we make the world."
— Buddha

This information about colleges, admissions, profiles, and lists is different in that it also provides unique tidbits. We hope you find this information valuable. Your job is to begin early by assembling information for the schools you are considering. Create a road map and set yourself on a clear path.

If you see an error in this book or even a suggestion for a future edition, please write to Dr. Rachel A. Winston at collegeguide@yahoo.com. We will fix the entry with the next printed version. All of that said, this book was written with you in mind.

There is a wealth of information on the Internet with free downloads, FAQs, testimonials, and offers to help you with your applications. Some of these advisors are knowledgeable and can help you. Students and parents hunt around the web, searching for a tremendous number of hours to seek the information they need. We aim to resolve this problem.

This book with college admissions data and profiles was designed to make your search easier. For now, though, we will assume you want to attend school for fashion merchandising and are exploring this avenue as a possible way to take advantage of a program to get you on your way toward your goal.

We assume that you are a talented candidate who is willing to work very hard. You may be fascinated with fashion, advertising, e-commerce, or retail management. Serving others selflessly is virtually a prerequisite for fashion merchandising programs.

As you investigate colleges, you might find that some programs are listed in different college departments; either way, this book will help you reach your goal. Applying to and writing essays for each application will require research to determine which is right for you.

While you might believe that fashion merchandising programs are relatively similar, each program's nuances make them very different. These small differences may seem confusing. My goal with this book is to demystify the information and process.

CONTENTS

Chapter 1: Fashion Sense: Discovering Outfits To Fit Individual Personalities — 1

Chapter 2: Retail and E-Commerce Industries: Industry Knowledge and Technology Skills To Master — 7

Chapter 3: Trends In Social Media and Eco-Friendly Purchases — 17

Chapter 4: Advertising and Marketing Skills: Business, Communication, and Graphic Design — 27

Chapter 5: Gaining Experience: Internships For High School, College, and beyond — 33

Chapter 6: What Is The Difference Between AA, AS, BA, BS, BFA, and MFA? — 45

Chapter 7: University Options: What College Programs Are Best For You? — 55

Chapter 8: College Admissions: Degrees, Coursework, Skills, and Scholarships — 63

Chapter 9: Post-Pandemic Employment Outlook: Statistics and Economic Projections — 75

Chapter 10: Next Steps: Preparation and Real-World Skills — 81

Chapter 11: Region One - Northeast 90

Chapter 12: Region Two - Midwest 104

Chapter 13: Region Three - South 122

Chapter 14: Region Four - West 154

Chapter 15: Fashion Merchandising Schools Alphabetized
by City/State 170

Chapter 16: Top 10 Fashion Merchandising Schools 174

Chapter 17: Fashion Merchandising Schools by Average
Test Score 176

Index 190

CHAPTER 1

FASHION SENSE: DISCOVERING OUTFITS TO FIT INDIVIDUAL PERSONALITIES

"Style is a way to say who you are without having to speak."

– **Rachel Zoe**

"LIFE IS A JOURNEY, NOT A DESTINATION."

Ralph Waldo Emerson suggested that people avoid conformity, search for an inner conscience, and discover a sense of purpose along the way. Enjoy your journey.

STYLE SPEAKS VOLUMES!

Everyone wears clothing. However, with the myriad of choices, how do individuals choose their personal brand or style? Literally, thousands of companies produce clothes of all shapes, colors, and prices. In addition, new t-shirt and accessories startups with low barriers to entry begin selling online every day. Some enterprising entrepreneurs start from scratch by creating a vision, brand, and platform. However, numerous successful brand names already dominate the market. Thus, the dynamic job of a fashion merchandiser is to translate clothing to the target market's tastes and personality.

With individuals seeking to keep up with the changing styles, the amount of new clothing purchased each year is staggering. In the past, people kept their clothing for years. However, in today's world, with the low cost of many items, many people throw away or give away their clothes and re-equip their wardrobe with new purchases. Furthermore, demand changes quickly, and outdated items are no longer necessary for new interests and environments. Thus, consumers see clothing as disposable, challenging fashion merchandisers to be continuously more inventive in their marketing strategies

Fashion merchandising is an exciting career with upward mobility and opportunities to think critically every day. However, navigating industry competition requires a certain *je ne sais quoi* attention to the three Ds: detail, data, and demand. New clothing startups begin in the e-commerce ecosystem with idea-generators and creatives hoping to make their mark on the marketplace. As these uniquely tailored companies start, they add a fresh face and a bit of innocence to a developed industry. Yet, with their bold entry, some inch closer to creating name recognition through innovative social media strategies while seeking to nab one of the top brand spots in the industry.

FROM ANTIQUITY, FASHION PLAYED A SIGNIFICANT ROLE IN SOCIETY

In Greek and Roman times, how a person dressed depicted their social status. People wore robes that matched their titles or roles. Certain colors were rare. For example, purple signified royalty, power, and wealth. Thousands of mollusks from the Phoenician city of Tyre (now Lebanon) were needed to make a gram of the purple color.

> Purple fabric used to be so outrageously expensive that only rulers could afford it… Since only wealthy rulers could afford to buy and wear the color, it became associated with the imperial classes of Rome, Egypt, and Persia. Purple also came to represent spirituality and holiness because the ancient emperors, kings and queens that wore the color were often thought of as gods or descendants of the gods.[1]

Other rare items, like gold and silver, adorned robes and crowns, which only the wealthy could afford. Specially tailored fabrics and designs, made for high-class individuals, were uniquely accessorized. Today, tailors still construct special occasion gowns for the rich and famous and small boutiques sell handcrafted apparel for those who can afford one-of-a-kind standout items.

INSPIRATION TO DISCOVERY TO PURCHASE

Fashion merchandisers have multiple roles. They must consider the latest trends, analyze the marketplace, and manage store layouts, price points, and design presentations. Inspiring a customer to purchase often means displaying

1   Remy Melina, "Why Is the Color Purple Associated with Royalty?," *Live Science*, Future US Inc, June 03, 2011, https://www.livescience.com/33324-purple-royal-color.html.

items online or in a retail store so that they can envision themselves in an outfit or don matching accessories. This discovery phase is essential since most customers do not know what they will buy before entering a retail store or online marketplace. They must be inspired to purchase by reading enticing text, communication, or imagery.

The following quote may inspire a customer to select a bold-colored scarf or a unique belt.

If you are not willing to risk the usual,

you will have to settle for the ordinary.

– Jim Rohn

This quote below might empower a woman to choose a men's jacket or a man to choose a bright yellow or pink shirt.

Style is knowing who you are,

what you want to say,

and not giving a damn.

– Gore Vidal

Meanwhile, fashion merchandising students study fashion as well as artistry, industry, business, and society. With this overview of topics, college programs provide the foundation for success, offering keys to an exciting and fascinating career.

PANDEMIC'S IMPACT

The pandemic changed the shape and size of every facet of the fashion industry. The quarantine threw the first curve. With civil unrest and anxiety, the summer of 2020 social justice movements leveled the second swerve. After initial surges of the pandemic, the economy and marketplace rode ups and downs as waves of customers ebbed and flowed. Jobs were lost to retail store closures, automation, and outsourcing. Nevertheless, in 2020, there were 90,500 employees in the U.S. apparel industry.[2]

According to the global consulting group McKinsey & Company, fashion companies increased profits by 4% in 2019, followed by a 90% drop in 2020.[3] McKinsey also noted that consumers were increasingly concerned with sustainability and commitment to fashion brand workers. Furthermore, 60% of customers believe that shopping with a mobile app is a factor in their brand decisions. *Forbes* states that mobile apps will comprise 73% of e-commerce sales in 2021.[4] Meanwhile, companies respond to their loyal purchasers by being flexible and adapting to demand.

---

2   M. Shahbandeh, "Number of Employees in the U.S. Apparel Manufacturing Industry from 1990 to 2020 (in 1,000s)," *Statista*, April 26, 2021, https://www.statista.com/statistics/242729/number-of-employees-in-theus-apparel-manufacturing-industry/.

3   Imran Amed et al., "State of Fashion 2022: An Uneven Recovery and New Frontiers," *McKinsey & Company*, December 1, 2021, https://www.mckinsey.com/industries/retail/our-insights/state-of-fashion.

4   Marc Porcelli, "Behind the Growth of Mobile Commerce," *Forbes*, June 25, 2021, https://www.forbes.com/sites/forbestechcouncil/2021/06/25/behind-the-growth-of-mobile-commerce/?sh=404471d8353b.

CHAPTER 2

RETAIL AND E-COMMERCE INDUSTRIES: INDUSTRY KNOWLEDGE AND TECHNOLOGY SKILLS TO MASTER

"Fashion is what you buy. Style is what you do with it."

– Anonymous

FASHION MERCHANDISING CAREER

F ashion merchandisers consider data, envision target markets, plan campaigns, advertise strategically, and promote sales. Fashion merchandisers make decisions about an apparel line for a specific season. They evaluate demand, select appropriate amounts, and manage sales. Therefore, statistical skills, accounting, and marketing training are a must. Visual displays and sales advertising comprise one component of fashion marketing, while the other involves apparel creation, supply chain management, product forecasting, budget creation, and distribution analysis. All of these comprise the encompassing business side of the job.

Fashion merchandisers must predict the future. The prognostications are aided by using past sales data, economic projections, global events, and experience with the fashion cycle. They must often plan four seasons ahead to forecast what trendy items people will want to purchase in the following year. This process requires envisioning volumes, products, styles, locations, and price points. After meeting with designers and laying out the merchandise they plan to sell, the wheels go into motion with the construction, manufacturing, distribution, showcasing, and sales.

The career opportunities in fashion merchandising have taken rollercoaster-like turns. Resilience is an essential skill with in-person retail's decline and online sale's rise. Specifically, e-commerce has experienced a significant market share increase. The "Forrester 2021 Online U.S. Retail Forecast" predicts that brick-and-mortar sales will rebound to take 71% of the retail sales by 2024, though changes are likely to take place.[1]

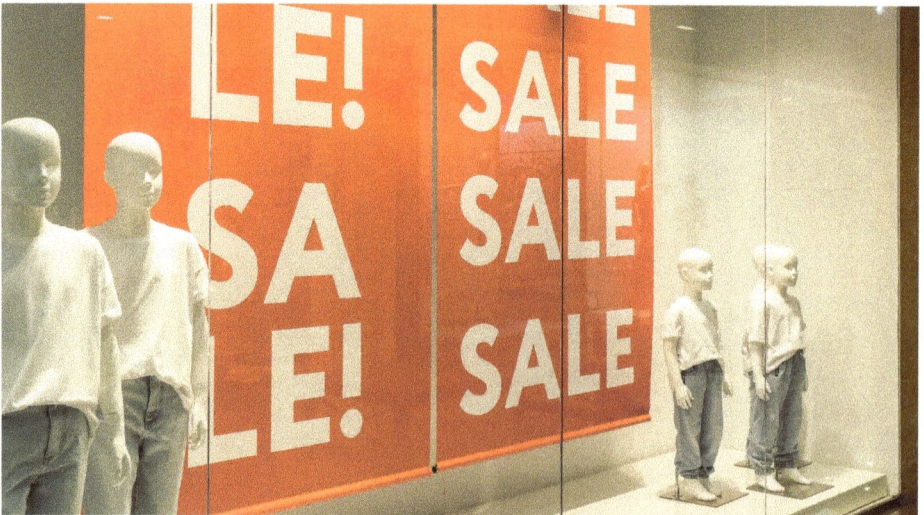

---

1   Dan Berthiaume, "Forrester: Stores Will Account for 71% of All U.S. Retail Sales by 2024," *Chain Store Age*, July 1, 2021, https://www.chainstoreage.com/forrester-stores-will-account-71-all-us-retail-sales-2024.

QUALITY, VALUE, AND PRICE

Understanding the consumer is the first step to success in this nearly $1.9 trillion industry. In the United States alone, sales of apparel, footwear, and accessories are expected to reach $500 billion. Who is buying? One-third of all sales are from Asia, while Europe commands the second-highest spot for apparel purchases. Additionally, the types of clothing demanded vary from country to country. Thus, mastering the analysis of consumer behavior, target personas, and quantitative modeling are essential.

When people vacation, celebrate, or go out, they tend to wear fun or luxury clothing. However, when families are hunkered down, they tend to be more casual and relaxed. Likewise, when people feel like they can spend money freely, they do not mind purchasing high-quality items, even when the clothing and accessories are significantly more expensive. Yet, when money is tight, individuals tend to spend much less. Furthermore, demand, like the post-pandemic increase in activewear purchases, drives customers to find the kinds of items they desire. Thus, personal income and lifestyle drive consumer demand.

Knowing the industry and company demographics is essential, as is studying statistics. Coresight Research released a report stating that in 2021, retailers would suffer the consequences of the continued pandemic with 10,000 store closures, a 14% increase from 2020.[2] Luxury and high fashion stores suffered the most. Meanwhile, grocery, dollar stores, and sports apparel markets survived tumultuous market adaptations. However, even these industries were impacted by fluctuations in workforce availability. Individual companies rode out the waves of highs and lows.

At the same time, numerous questions arose. What socioeconomic groups tend to buy from a specific brand? How can quality, value, or price entice these individuals?

Boutique stores cannot compete with the prices large companies charge since they buy in volume. However, they can be very successful in more localized communities with one-of-a-kind items that large retailers do not sell. Thus, education in fashion merchandising is more than just knowing what people like but how to locate target customers.

---

2   Coresight Research, "US and UK Store Closures Review 2020 and US Outlook 2021," *Coresight Research*, January 28, 2021, https://coresight.com/research/us-and-uk-store-closures-review-2020-and-us-outlook-2021/.

BRAND COMPETITION

Individuals typically migrate to the same brands time after time because they know what they will get, and they like how they feel in those clothes. So, how does the fashion merchandiser get a customer's attention to try a different brand and attract them to their apparel? What drives a purchaser online or to an outlet store if they traditionally purchase from a luxury brand storeroom. You will learn this in college. Suffice it to say that with nearly 100,000 apparel stores in the United States, the landscape of fashion brands is highly competitive.

In the United States, the fifty largest companies hold approximately 70% of the market share. Breaking into this space is tough. Success depends upon merchandising, advertising, and marketing. The goal is for companies to effectively capitalize on their target market. Customer service is essential.

According to Brand Finance, the top 50 fashion brands in 2021 are:

1. Nike (USA)
2. Gucci (Italy)
3. Louis Vuitton (France)
4. Adidas (Germany)
5. Chanel (France)
6. Zara (Spain)
7. Uniqlo (Japan)
8. H&M (Sweden)
9. Cartier (France)
10. Hermes (France)
11. Rolex (Switzerland)
12. Dior (France)

13. Tiffany & Co. (USA)
14. Chow Tai Fook (China)
15. COACH (USA)
16. The North Face (USA)
17. Anta (China)
18. Victoria's Secret (USA)
19. Omega (Switzerland)
20. Puma (Germany)
21. Burberry (Great Britain)
22. Ralph Lauren (USA)
23. Ray-Ban (Italy)
24. Levi's (USA)
25. Lululemon (Canada)
26. Prada (Italy)
27. Bulgari (Italy)
28. Old Navy (USA)
29. Under Armour (USA)
30. Moncler (Italy)
31. Michael Kors (USA)
32. Yves Saint Laurent (France)
33. Fila (South Korea)
34. Next (United Kingdom)
35. Primark/Penneys (Ireland)
36. Tommy Hilfiger (USA)
37. Pandora (Danish)
38. Calvin Klein (USA)
39. Armani (Italy)
40. Givenchy (France)
41. Lao Feng Xiang (China)
42. Skechers (USA)
43. TAG Heuer (Switzerland)
44. New Balance (USA)
45. Valentino (Italy)
46. Hugo Boss (Germany)
47. Converse (USA)
48. Timberland (USA)
49. Loewe (Spain)
50. Bosideng (China)

By knowing the industry and using data-informed decision-making, fashion merchandisers serve customers by providing them with what they demand in a way that serves the public and the company. Education, training, and work experiences serve as a foundation for a rewarding career.

PANDEMIC EMERGENCE: NO MORE BOREDOM

During the quarantine and lingering pandemic, people became bored with their clothing. Seeking uniqueness and style, individuals hunted for multicolored flair, fringe, puffy clothes, jumpsuits, bell-bottoms, and cutout garments. The vibrancy of color surprised those who became used to neutral colors and pajama pants.

Fall 2021 began the new wave of tiny trendy fashion apparel. "Meet the micro-mini skirt, a holdover from the going-out styles of the early to mid-aughts, worn by all the biggest names of that era: Paris Hilton, Nicole Richie, Britney Spears, and Lindsay Lohan among them. The style re-emerged and began picking up steam on the runways earlier this year, when Miu Miu and Saint Laurent showed teeny skirts in embellished jewels and tweeds for fall 2021."[3]

FASHION MERCHANDISING FOR THE METAVERSE

The metaverse added a new dimension for the fashion merchandiser. According to *Forbes*, in 2022, video game skins offer fashion designers a $40 billion per year market space.[4] Creativity and flair will allow image creators to wow. While

---

3   https://www.wmagazine.com/fashion/micro-mini-skirt-y2k-fashion-mcbling-history

4   Joseph DeAcetis, "NFTs, Metaverse and GameFi Are Changing Up the Fashion Business in 2022," *Forbes*, December 22, 2021, https://www.forbes.com/sites/josephdeacetis/2021/12/22/nfts-metaverse-and-gamefi-are-changing-up-the-fashion-business-in-2022/.

the trifecta of demand, software, and hardware are converging in the 3D video space, the metaverse stands prepared to change the way we live and work.

According to Grayscale Investments, the world's largest crypto asset manager, "The market opportunity for bringing the Metaverse to life may be worth over $1 trillion in annual revenue and may compete with Web 2.0 companies worth ~$15 trillion in market value today."[5] While the metaverse may seem futuristic and sci-fi-like, billions of people are flocking to this new space. Meanwhile, video games and the Internet are likely to be transformed into this new 3D universe.

Numbers tell the story. Digital entertainment is a vast market with statistics that surpass prognosticators projections. According to *FinancesOnline*, "There were 2.69 billion video game players worldwide in 2020. The figure will rise to 3.07 billion in 2023 based on a 5.6% year-on-year growth forecast. The global games market had $159.3 billion in revenues for 2020, almost half of which came from the Asia Pacific market."[6]

To put this into perspective. One-third of the global population plays video games. While approximately two-thirds of residents in the United States play video games, this only comprises 15% of global gamers. What does this mean for digital creatives? If 85% of gamers live in other countries, geographical knowledge, cultural sensitivity, language acquisition will become increasingly valuable assets. There is a massive space for fashion designers with graphic design and advanced technology skills to jump on board. Furthermore, these numbers are destined to grow.

Generation Z and Millennials are investing in their virtual skill sets. Additionally, this group from 15 to 35 is expected to spend a trillion dollars on these technologies between 2022 and 2027. The once generic avatar skins and digital clothing styles are rapidly adapting to the new environment with styles that can quickly be updated from season to season. Creating personalized spaces, styles, and clothing, the metaverse's virtually enhanced physical and digital environment is set to provide social connections, amplifying the universe of the Internet. Video game and metaverse avatars will have personalized clothing without the need for manufacturing – a real game-changer, pardon the pun.

---

5   Michael Cohen, "Grayscale Says Metaverse Tech Sector May Generate $1T Annual Revenue in the Future," *MSN, Microsoft News*, November 28, 2021, https://www.msn.com/en-us/money/news/grayscale-says-metaverse-tech-sector-may-generate-1t-annual-revenue-in-the-future/ar-AARe6nZ.

6   "Number of Gamers Worldwide 2022/2023: Demographics, Statistics, and Predictions," *FinancesOnline*, accessed January 28, 2022, https://financesonline.com/number-of-gamers-worldwide/.

14

The environment is primed to attract customers to your differentiated digital fashion brand. Big-name fashion brands like Dior, Gucci, Prada, Armani, and Miu Miu are some of the few companies with avatar branded garments. In addition, the video game, Fortnite, partnered with Balenciaga while Louis Vuitton partnered with League of Legends. Partnerships will increase as this avenue becomes more common. Popular virtual fashion specialists include XR Couture, The Fabricant, and DressX. Fashion brands are eager to attract young customers who will stay with them for life.

Marketing skills will become much more important to next-gen fashion designers as they target audiences to their business's core values. Consumer connectedness, social consciousness, and brand awareness will be even more important in these new digital environments. The creative and financial opportunities are virtually limitless. Fashion designers and fashion Merchandisers now have wide-ranging freedom to bring their fashions to life – literally. Along with a combination of cryptocurrencies and non-fungible tokens (NFTs), the purchasing power of Gen Zs and Millennials will drive the fashion train into the next station – the metaverse.

FASHION MERCHANDISERS WITH TECHNOLOGY SKILLS APPLY HERE

The fashion industry needs skilled workers. Technological skills continue to be in high demand. Companies search long and hard for applicants to fashion merchandising jobs who also have digital marketing, cybersecurity, supply chain logistics, wearable technology, and STEM skills. To recover from the past few years of downturns, brands must upgrade and update their deliverables and enter the next frontier of digitization. Inflation and price increases will change industry dynamics. Competition for the best and brightest applicants with technology skills has never been greater.

"LIFE IS A JOURNEY, NOT A DESTINATION"

Ralph Waldo Emerson suggested that people avoid conformity, search for an inner conscience, and discover a sense of purpose along the way. Enjoy your journey.

CHAPTER 3

TRENDS IN SOCIAL MEDIA AND ECO-FRIENDLY PURCHASES

"Cheap fashion is really far from that, it may be cheap in terms of the financial cost, but very expensive when it comes to the environment and the cost of human life."

– Sass Brown

SOCIAL MEDIA AND TREND SHOPPING

Skills to Know: *Economics, Psychology, Consumer Behavior, Marketing*

Influencers have a significant say in market demand. Social media icons with hundreds of thousands of followers engage readers in discussing brand quality, price, sustainability, accountability, new designs, and fair treatment of employees. Studying these systems in college offers the chance to gain a global view of past and present trends.

Consumer behavior drives investment. This infusion of money, in turn, spurs on technology development like in-app purchases and integrated augmented reality, allowing potential purchasers to try on items and test out products. Seamless online shopping experiences encourage purchasing, while artificial intelligence highlights items for customers by preference choices. As a result, there is significant potential for industry growth.

SUSTAINABLE, RECYCLABLE, AND REUSABLE

Skills to Know: *Environmental Science, Sustainability, Design*

The greater global consciousness surrounding eco-friendly consumer products caught the fashion industry by storm, accelerating in 2022 with concepts like vegan leather, mushroom leather, slow fashion, ethical manufacturing, and second-hand clothing. Organic fabrics appeal to an individual's values. As an alternative to quick purchase wear and fast fashion, Ethical garments, like Eileen Fisher, hold a brand allure as people look for ways to protect the environment, protect workers, and ensure inclusivity. Stella McCartney's materials include recycled and natural fabrics.

Another trend in consumer purchasing is recycling and sustainability tags. Students may want to research and investigate the implementation of environmentally sound sales before an admissions or job interview, if the college or company offers one.

Cheaply made, fast fashion puts the planet at risk with its polymer-derived microplastics, synthetic fibers, and chemically-infused fabrics. When clothing is washed or heated, chemicals and plastics enter our water lines and damage our ecosystem. Thus, the term "sustainable" is not synonymous with clean or fresh, but tantamount to materials made with natural fibers and non-toxic fabrics throughout the material production and garment lifecycle. Recycling has also become increasingly popular.

Lightly worn garments are the latest in a growing trend. Second-hand shops are growing online and in brick-and-mortar stores. Closed-loop recycling offers a sustainable option to reduce the use of raw material extraction and production, decrease landfill waste, and increase the creativity involved in reimagining style and product development from previously crafted items. With the growing number of second-hand stores, shoppers have a wide selection of unique clothing items.

PRODUCT PASSPORTS

Skills to Know: *Economics, Business, Human Resources, Social Issues*

Fashion companies are rolling out RFID chips and product labeling to let purchasers know the brand sustainability quotient, raw materials used, commitment to employees (diversity, healthcare, fair wages), and corporate standards. Customer's desire to know more has also driven companies to be transparent online regarding their corporate practices. On the business side, brands will be better able to determine product authenticity, prevent counterfeiting, and create an environment of loyalty, consciousness, and trustworthiness.

This escalating trend includes digital IDs like QR codes, NFC embedded tags, and RFID chips as well as non-digital biodegradable labels. Sustainability labeling offers an awareness and accountability tool, providing information about the fabric – authenticity, water usage, carbon footprint, location/date where the garment was produced, employer treatment, supply chain, the longevity of wear, even identifying the flock of sheep where the wool was shorn and its vaccinations. These traceable identifiers are not yet uniformly formatted, but, one day, they are likely to have universal requirements like food labels.

B CORP CERTIFICATION

The B Corp model is to re-imagine this century's commitment to sustainability. With the goal to generate profit while helping the planet, B Corp's undergo a rigorous certification process, comprehensive assessment, and verification of social and environmental performance. B Corp Certification is a third-party evaluation on all stakeholders from the B Lab, "the nonprofit network transforming the global economy to benefit all people, communities, and the planet." [1]

---

1   B Lab, "About," *B Lab,* n.d., https://www.bcorporation.net/en-us/movement/about-b-lab

The definition of a B Corp is:

> Certified B Corporations are businesses that meet the highest
> standards of verified social and environmental performance, public
> transparency, and legal accountability to balance profit and purpose.
> B Corps are accelerating a global culture shift to redefine success in
> business and build a more inclusive and sustainable economy.

The fashion industry's commitment to sustainability drove companies to
seek ways they could be more eco-friendly and purposeful, while reducing global
inequity. To generate and promote better business practices, companies and
organizations banded to meet high standards of environmental consciousness
and social accountability. B Corps fashion brands are given grades based on their
commitment to ensuring an inclusive, sustainable economy.

Some companies like Cotopaxi, donate a percentage of their revenue to
end poverty and their employees commit a percentage of their paid work time
volunteering in their community. Meanwhile, service-oriented companies, like
Tentree's Earth-First commitment, planting ten trees for every purchase. Tentree
makes choices "where the planet and its people come first, always. Tentree's goal
is to reach 1 billion trees by 2030".[2] Similarly, companies like Allbirds, Patagonia,
Frank and Oak, Bombas, and United By Blue commit to environmental sensitivity.

2   Tentree, "About," *Tentree,* n.d., https://www.tentree.com/pages/about

PROFILE: PATAGONIA[3]

Patagonia's Mission Statement: We're In Business To Save Our Home Planet.

Our Reason For Being
At Patagonia, we appreciate that all life on earth is under threat of extinction. We aim to use the resources we have—our business, our investments, our voice and our imaginations—to do something about it.

Build The Best Product
Our criteria for the best product rests on function, repairability, and, foremost, durability. Among the most direct ways we can limit ecological impacts is with goods that last for generations or can be recycled so the materials in them remain in use. Making the best product matters for saving the planet.

Cause No Unnecessary Harm
We know that our business activity—from lighting stores to dyeing shirts—is part of the problem. We work steadily to change our business practices and share what we've learned. But we recognise that this is not enough. We seek not only to do less harm, but more good.

Use Business To Protect Nature
The challenges we face as a society require leadership. Once we identify a problem, we act. We embrace risk and act to protect and restore the stability, integrity and beauty of the web of life.

Not Bound By Convention
Our success—and much of the fun—lies in developing new ways to do things.

---

3   Patagonia, "Our Mission," *Patagonia,* n.d., https://www.patagonia.com.au/pages/our-mission

CARBON FOOTPRINT AND ENVIRONMENTAL SUSTAINABILITY

The United Nations called on the fashion industry to lessen its environmental impact, promote sustainable consumption, reach its Sustainable Development Goals, follow the UN Framework Convention on Climate Change, and commit to the Paris Climate Agreement. As the need for sustainability becomes more urgent, innovation, digitization, reuse, pollution, and logistics will be the key topics of conversation. Industry leaders have called for eco-conscience transparency with the goal of a net-zero environmental impact.

The apparel industry is one of the biggest polluters on the planet. Textile mills generate one-fifth of the world's industrial water pollution and use 20,000 chemicals, many of them carcinogenic, to make clothes. Chinese textile factories alone produce about three billion tons of soot—air pollution linked to respiratory and heart disease—every year by burning coal for energy. Most of the world's textile factories are in developing countries where governments can't keep pace with the industry's massive pollution footprint.[4]

The textile industry
1. produces global greenhouse gas emissions from the incineration of clothing
2. manufactures garments made with microplastics
3. leaves untreated toxic pollution
4. creates wastelands of landfills
5. transports tons of clothing in damaging supply chain operations
6. responsible for harmful chemicals in dyes, pesticides, and detergents

Container ships filled with fashion industry garments travel from low-labor-cost countries like Bangladesh, China, India, Indonesia, and the Philippines to first-world countries every day. At the end of the life cycle, waste appears in countries willing to accept vessels containing fast-fashion discards. "The global fashion industry produces over 92 million tonnes of waste per year. In the U.S. alone, over 17 million tons of used textile waste are generated annually." For example, 39,000 tons of discarded clothing fill Chile's desert. Furthermore, a quarter of global CO_2 emissions come from the transportation industry, which is projected to double by 2050 with e-commerce leading the way.

4   NDRC, "Encourage Textile Manufacturers to Reduce Pollution," *NDRC*, n.d., https://www.nrdc.org/issues/encourage-textile-manufacturers-reduce-pollution

As the fashion industry's carbon footprint expands, environmental sustainability practices are even more important. Circular use of garments from growth to decay needs to begin with raw material production. Textile producers need to lead the way encouraged by fashion brands.

THE FUTURE OF THE FASHION INDUSTRY

Tornados whipped through the fashion and beauty industry as companies were swept into mergers, acquisitions, and partnerships. With small companies rising and medium-sized companies whisked into the winds of change, environmental consciousness rises to the top of the wind tunnel. In the swirl to offer consumers 'ethical' wardrobes, some companies are in a race to find new eco-friendly threads and fabric while also pointing themselves toward artificial intelligence and augmented reality to convey their message.

NATURAL TEXTILE FIBRES

COTTON

LINEN

BAMBOO

HEMP

WOOL

SILK

SYNTHETIC TEXTILE FIBRES

ELASTANE

ARAMID

NYLON

ACRYLIC

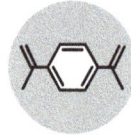
POLYESTER

PU LEATHER

THE RACE FOR BIO-DEGRADABLE TEXTILES

Many synthetic textile fibers are not biodegradable and could take more than a century to decompose. This situation caused brands to hunt for new fibers as consumers ask how much of an environmental impact is the clothing going to cost in the long run from farming and processing to production and shipping. Fabrics made from cotton, silk, and hemp are household names, but you might be surprised at fashions made from apples, pineapple, and cork.

Sustainable Jungle offers this list of sustainable fabrics.

Sustainable Natural and Vegan Fabrics

Bamboo Linen	Organic Cotton	Recycled Cotton
Cork	Organic Hemp	
Organic Bamboo	Organic Linen	

Vegan, Synthetic Fabrics

Econyl	Recycled Polyester

Sustainable Semi-Synthetic Fabrics (mostly vegan)

Apple Leather	Lyocell	Scoby Leather
Bamboo Lyocell	Modal	S.Cafe
Brewed Protein	Pinatex	Woocoo
Cupro	QMilk	
EcoVero	Qmonos	

Animal Derived Natural Fabrics (sustainable depending on source)

Alpaca Wool	Down	Silk
Camel	Merino Wool	Vegetable Tanned Leather
Cashmere	Sheep Wool	Yak Wool

Fashion designers will be on the cutting edge of creating the next wave of sustainable textiles. Meanwhile, fashion merchandisers will be hard at work articulating and marketing eco-friendly products to this environmentally conscious generation. This moment in history can be defined by a dramatic transformation in the way we live, the way we work, and the clothing we choose to wear.

"There is no beauty in the finest cloth if it makes hunger and unhappiness" – Mahatma Gandhi

CHAPTER 4

ADVERTISING AND MARKETING SKILLS: BUSINESS, COMMUNICATION, AND GRAPHIC DESIGN

"I've learned that people will forget what you said, people will forget what you did, but people will never forget how you made them feel."

– Maya Angelou

MAKING PEOPLE FEEL GREAT DURING A CRISIS

"Hello! How may I help you?"

The personal touch means everything to people who have little contact with others. Many people are lonely. They once spent time with friends and family. While surveys say that people appreciate quick online shopping, they also feel distant and separated from people. So, how do you make people feel great during a time of crisis?

People once met at restaurants, theatres, pools, and malls. Now, they only hear an automated robot that says, "Stay on the line for the next available operator… Sorry for the long delays. We are doing everything we can to help you."

Compassion and understanding go a long way in making a person's day. By studying fashion merchandising, you will also study advertising and marketing. Those who can combine the personalization and compassion people desire with the service and value they expect will be truly successful. In addition, fashion merchandising students will pave a new avenue toward the transition to post-COVID methods with new and innovative marketing techniques.

Innovative thinkers who have great communication skills along with talents in graphic design will be able to communicate messages effectively with images and text. Mastering Adobe Photoshop, Illustrator, and InDesign will add value to the skills you learn in a fashion marketing program. The marketplace is competitive, so any additional skills you obtain will increase your ability to sell yourself to the brand of your dreams.

COMMUNICATING VALUE AND QUALITY

Coming out of the pandemic in 2022 and beyond, fashion merchandisers needed to quickly recognize fundamental marketplace shifts. In particular, the lockdowns and mandates meant being nimble and prepared for change. The quarantine forced people to work from home. Changes in family life required a more complex digital ecosystem, which meant that the Internet and technology needed to be shared. Often family members worked at different times of the day to take advantage of greater bandwidth. However, the pandemic also drove styles toward relaxed clothing, waist-up attire to complement digital backgrounds, and activewear for walking, biking, meditation, and exercise.

Emerging from the pandemic, consumers remained fiscally cautious. While most purchasers moved online, their needs changed. They desired comfort in their homes and lives. In caring for their health, most people became more conscious of their lifestyle. In creating mental and physical wellbeing, most individuals have taken a mindfulness approach, searching for ways to improve their positivity in the face of the crisis. Seeking self-care and stress reduction, many individuals chose a more casual, minimalist fashion style in the comfort of their home. Thus, for the fashion merchandiser, considering how people have changed their lives and sought low-cost, easily accessible, quality products the landscape of advertising and marketing fashion has changed.

In addition to fashion sense, fashion merchandising also requires a considerable understanding of quality, value, and price-points for targeted customers. Fashion merchandisers need new ways of thinking about products. How can a campaign be designed so that products give consumers a sense of spontaneity, soul, love, freedom, liveliness, energy, agility, lightness, safety, longevity, and self-care? Especially with those hit hard financially, fashion merchandisers must internalize (1) each product's price-value relationship, (2) the customer's desire to get more for less, and (3) the necessity to save money without sacrificing quality. These keys to understanding a customer's willingness to purchase provide the foundation for spending decisions in the midst of lingering crises.

BRICK-AND-MORTAR TO E-COMMERCE MARKETPLACE

Amazon took the e-marketplace by storm during the pandemic. However, Google was also a big winner with people stranded in their homes. The Internet was one of the only places to buy and sell goods. As a result, the retail marketplace nearly collapsed. While brick-and-mortar stores had suffered for years due to consumer shifts to e-commerce, the pandemic was the final straw for many retailers. Others teetered on the brink. Though Chapter 11 is not necessarily the end of the road, the milestone is significant.

A few 2021 Chapter 11 filings include:[1]

Lorna Jane: Australian activewear retailer (filed September 2021)

Sequential Brands Group: Jessica Simpson, Joe's Jeans, Avia, and AND1 (filed August 2021)

Global Brands Group USA: All Saints, Saga, and Le Tigre wholesaling to Macy's Nordstrom, Bloomingdales, and Costco (filed July 2021)

Alex and Ani: Jewelry brand known for bangle bracelets (filed June 2021)

The Collected Group: Brand labels Joie, Current/Elliot, and Equipment (filed April 2021)

Solstice Marketing Concepts: Sunglasses (February 2021)

L'Occitane: French beauty retailer (January 2021)

---

1   CB Insights, "Here's A List Of 135 Bankruptcies In The Retail Apocalypse – And Why They Failed," *CB Insights,* September 29, 2021, https://www.cbinsights.com/research/retail-apocalypse-timeline-infographic/#2021.

CHANGES IN THE RETAIL FASHION LANDSCAPE

Retail stores could no longer pay rent and customers no longer came in droves to retail stores. As a result, underperforming stores shuttered, pivoting corporate focuses out of enclosed malls and onto the web. With two Christmas seasons down and very little foot traffic, fashion merchandisers had to rethink the marketplace and find new avenues to make their mark.

Demand changed too. With fewer people going to offices, professional clothing, like suits, ties, and professional women's wear, lost traction in exchange for work-from-home comfort clothing, sportswear, and smart clothing. Fashion merchandisers need to be able to see trends, like the casualization of apparel. Smart casual, leisurewear, even in professional environments, a trend that began before the pandemic, is now prevalent across industries and corporate offices as people slowly return to workplaces.

Even the design of retail stores will need to change due to consumer demand for quick purchases with less exposure to other customers, fueled by concerns about risk, fear, uncertainties, and short tempers of people who have little patience. Convenience shopping is the new mantra, along with touch-free curbside pick-ups. Marketers will need to reassess how to encourage shoppers to buy that one extra item they did not know they needed if they are not going into a store. The pandemic changed advertising, promotion, and sales in significant ways. Fashion marketers will need to be flexible in the face of continued changes.

CHAPTER 5

GAINING EXPERIENCE: INTERNSHIPS FOR HIGH SCHOOL, COLLEGE, AND BEYOND

"The purpose of education is to enable us to develop to the fullest that which is inside us."

— **Norman Cousins**

UNLOCK THE DOOR: STEP INSIDE

Internships are the key to unlocking the fashion industry's door. Enter! The exciting next step through the door of opportunity is the beginning of your remarkable career. Awaiting you on the other side is a thrilling adventure. Don't let the modern interior spaces and beautiful décor catch you off-guard, there is a swirling wind of activity inside and a 100-mph storm. While problem-solving is essential, you will never be bored.

Get off to a good start by being organized. Start looking long before you want to begin. Just like college applications, which must be submitted six to ten months ahead of time, begin planning ahead of time for internships. If you are considering a summer internship, you should start searching during your winter break. Applications frequently open at the beginning of the new year for summer internships. The deadlines close earlier than you may expect. Create a digital or hard copy calendar system that works for you with dates, deadlines, contacts, interviews, and networking opportunities.

Note that internships may be posted at your school or on websites and social media. You will not be the only one poised to jump in and get a head start. Companies become inundated with requests for more information, applications, and follow-up calls. If you know of someone in the organization to whom you can send your information first or who could follow up on your behalf, contact them, explaining that you are interested in a summer internship.

A FEW SUMMER PROGRAMS FOR HIGH SCHOOL STUDENTS

Columbus College of Art & Design Fashion Design Workshop – Columbus, OH: 1-week pattern drafting, sewing construction, and design.

Drexel University Design, Merchandising, and Fashion Program – Philadelphia, PA: 2-week fashion design program with field trips and portfolio preparation.

Fashion Design & Sewing Camp – NYC: 1 and 2-week programs include the business side of the fashion industry

Fashion Institute of Design & Merchandising – LA, OC, SD, California: 3 Days of Fashion – Crash course in design, draping, and marketing.

Fashion Institute of Technology – NYC: Pre-College Fashion Forecasting, Fashion Journalism, Costume & Couture

LIM College Fashion Lab Program – NYC: 4-week Business of Fashion program includes fashion photography, celebrity styling, event planning and marketing communications

Parson's School of Design Summer Intensive Studies Program – Paris and NYC: 2 and 4-week "boot camps"

Pratt Pre-College Fashion Classes – Manhattan & Brooklyn: 4-week Fashion Program

Rhode Island School of Design Pre-College Program – Providence, RI: 6-week residential program Fashion Design

Savannah College of Art and Design Pre-College Rising Star Program – Savannah, CA: 5-week portfolio development and design skills

School of the Arts Institute of Chicago: 3-week summer arts/portfolio institute – Priority Scholarship deadline March 1

Summer Discovery Fashion Design – UCLA: 3-week program

Summer Discovery Fashion Academy – Austin, TX : The University of Texas at Austin - 3-week program

Teen Vogue **and Parson's School of Design** – Online Summer Program

The School of the New York Times: Summer Fashion Academy – New York City and Washington, D.C.: Two weeks (NYC program on the Future of Fashion)

The University of Texas at Austin – McCombs Future Executive Academy: Free, No Tuition

USE YOUR COLLEGE EXPERIENCE TO OPEN DOORS

College can be challenging, rigorous, and exhilarating. While there are tons of projects and opportunities, do not squander your time. Instead, use some of your precious minutes to find an internship. If you have a project in a fashion merchandising class to interview someone, choose an industry professional you admire and make a connection. Connect with people in the industry and network while in college. Gain experience. Any experience is a start. Build on every step you take. Your first moments in the fast-paced fashion industry may be tough, scary, and challenging, but take advantage of the opportunity.

SKILLS

You are now on the hunt to locate the doors you want to open and the keys to unlock the door. While internships are difficult to obtain, you need to have the required skills. Build these ahead of time. Look through the fashion industry job descriptions that seem most interesting. Take classes that enhance your technical, website, or social media skills ahead of time. Then, when you are writing your resume and cover letter, include your skills and capabilities.

Writing skills are valuable. One option is for you to take your first step in this industry by writing a personal fashion blog or conducting research on a fashion merchandising company. You might want to try fashion journalism by writing articles, photographing trending looks, or creating your own designs and sending articles to a magazine.

EXCELLENT COLLEGE/UNIVERSITY FASHION MAGAZINES

Columbia University – *Hoot Magazine*

Connecticut College – *The LOOK Magazine*

Fashion Institute of Design and Merchandising – *FIDM Mode*

Fashion Institute of Technology – *Blush Magazine*

Lasell College – *Polished Magazine*

Michigan State University – *VIM Magazine*

New York University – *Fringe Magazine*

Northwestern University – *STITCH Magazine*

Ohio University – *Thread Magazine*

Parson's School of Design – *re:D (Regarding Design)*

Rutgers University – **Trim Magazine**
Southern Methodist University – **SMU LOOK**
Stanford University – **MINT Magazine**
Syracuse University – **Zipped Magazine**
University of California, Berkeley – **Bare**
University of Michigan **– SHEI Magazine**
University of Pennsylvania **– The Walk**
University of Wisconsin-Madison **– Moda**

MAJOR FASHION MAGAZINES

303 – Denver, CO
AnOther Magazine – United Kingdom
Attire Club – Vienna, Australia
Business of Fashion – London, England
Cliché Magazine – Las Vegas, NV
Design Scene – Europe
E! Online – Hollywood, CA
Elle – New York, NY
Fashion Network – Online
Femina – India
Fibre2Fashion – Ahmedabad, Gujarat, India
Harper's BAZAAR – New York, NY
i-D Fashion – London, England
I Knock Fashion – Online
InStyle – New York, NY
Marie Claire – New York, NY
Taylor & Francis Online – Abingdon, England, UK
Vogue Magazine – New York, NY
W Magazine – New York, NY
Who What Wear – Online
Women's Wear Daily – Online

COMPETITION

There are more than fifty people for every one position – even the unpaid internships. The fashion industry is competitive. Some hopeful interns networked, helped industry workers, offered free designs, edited articles, and carried out significant tasks. These actions happened long before they walked through the glamorous doors. Many potential interns are willing to do extra tasks to find that magical key.

Merely sending in a resume will not get you very far. You need to show initiative. Passively sending a resume and cover letter does not show much drive or desire. No matter what skills you have, persistence, determination, commitment, desire, and hunger are essential in the fashion industry. Your resume and cover letter are very likely to evaporate into the ether if you send it into cyberspace.

Do not apply to only one internship unless you know the person who is choosing the intern, and you are guaranteed a position. There could be hundreds of applicants. If you are determined to get an internship, apply to a few. Since there is no certainty, even if you are by far the best candidate, the process can be arduous and frustrating but worth the effort.

REFERENCES AND CHECKS

In the final rounds, companies will check your references and may call the people you chose to refer you. Follow up with your recommenders. Make sure you back up your resume experiences regarding club membership, education, and certificates. Finally, look over your social media accounts, even those you do not list on your resume or cover letter. Company human resource representatives are likely to look you up on Instagram, Twitter, Facebook, YouTube, Vimeo, Pinterest, etc. Make sure that you have touched all bases regarding images, text, appropriateness, responses, etc.

RESUMES AND COVER LETTERS

Many people use resume and cover letter templates. The benefit is speed and a sense of going in the right direction. However, these tend to be generic, even if your substance is unique. If you cannot format the resume to the required specifications or in a professionally appropriate way, create one from scratch, have someone help you create the resume, or go into your career center to have an expert give you some guidance. Either way, your job is to stand out and not look like every other applicant.

Neither your resume nor your cover letter should be more than one page. Few busy people will ever look at the second page. If a page is placed on a desk, employers rarely turn the page over or flip to other pages. Thus, for your resume, your job is to clearly and neatly display your background on one page. Make sure that you include any experience in the fashion industry, including retail, design, journalism, or photography. If you took related classes or participated in fashion clubs, include these. For your cover letter, make sure you read the job description and include your relevant skills along with evidence that you understand the company's mission, vision, and values.

JOB APPLICATIONS

Read the application announcement carefully. Follow the instructions. If they do not want a resume, do not include one. If they want a photograph, make sure you provide the image in the format they want. If they want a sample of your art, designs, or writing, deliver the type and amount as specified. There are almost always instructions. For example, applicants may be instructed to send attachments via WeTransfer or DropBox instead of via email. Read these notations first so that your application does not get thrown out from the start. Also, make sure to write the subject line of any e-mail as specified. Otherwise, the e-mail may be automatically deleted or sent to spam.

INTERVIEWS

The company will need to discover what you are like to work with in person. Even if some of your work is remote, your personality can shine through during in-person and virtual interviews. The image you present provides the company with an essential impression as to what you might look and act like in their offices. As you prepare, keep the company's corporate culture in mind – trendy, streetwear, business casual, suits, dresses, boots, all black, all white, or all pink.

Search the brand. View online images of the company's employees as the work in stores, offices, or trade shows. If you wear your favorite cashmere sweater or a St. John or Chanel suit, no matter how stylish you believe you appear, the look may be inappropriate for the company's fashion ensemble image.

You may be offered an individual interview, a group interview, or one that is online and asynchronous. In the last type, the company will send you a link to questions, and you will record and return your video answers.

JOB RESPONSIBILITIES

Every internship is different. During your first internship, you may be offered opportunities to sit in on meetings, provide suggestions, and contribute to big decisions. Each responsibility you are given is a step in the right direction. You will review, edit, design, produce content, manage tasks, and do whatever is required to quicken the delivery of the next project. The pace of work can often be likened to a tornado of duties – demanding, exhausting, and thrilling at the same time.

You also may be given tasks no bigger than pouring coffee, delivering paperwork, or wrapping boxes. These may seem trivial or inconsequential, but they are equally important in the big picture of the operation. Someone needs to do them and you are lowest on the totem pole. Do not feel bad. Your supervisor may just be testing you to see if you have a good attitude. Bad attitudes are easy to spot. Additionally, you can learn much from observing other people and how they act. Take in the surroundings. If you are an efficient, positive, and supportive intern, you may land one of the future coveted openings.

Work ethic is essential. Certain expectations come with the territory – come early, leave late, do extra work, and provide value. Without delivering these extra benefits to the company, you will find it difficult to get the good reference you will need to open the next bigger door. After all, your value begins when you relieve your supervisor's stress, complete all of the tasks, and also produce income.

SALARY

Most internships are unpaid. Unless you have previous experience specifically in the fashion industry, you are a trainee. You have much to learn. Consider your first internship as a training program since you are literally learning how to work independently. Your value begins when you produce income for the company. In the beginning, the tempo, day-to-day responsibilities, and unspoken expectations can be stressful. Your first fashion merchandising position offers a frame of reference – a step into a fast-paced and glamorous world.

Once you have your first internship, your second internship will allow you to take a few more steps forward. If this second internship is unpaid, look at this as an opportunity to learn new skills. Remember, attitude is everything. Ask your supervisor for additional tasks, while taking more responsibility, gaining greater independence, and networking with staff throughout the company.

However, there are also paid internships. Depending upon your experience, skillset, and focus, paid internships can range from minimum wage to $30 per hour.

INTERNSHIP OPPORTUNITIES

One basic but most direct way to find an internship is on a company's website. These postings include the jobs, requirements, and applications. There is no fee and less concern that your information will be sold to other companies. The open jobs are listed. Occasionally, websites are out of date, but human resource officers are generally very good about keeping current and providing a direct application path with clarity about those that are outdated or closed.

The most direct way to find an internship is on a company's website. Postings include job titles, requirements, and applications. The company does not charge a fee, and, unlike outside services, your information is unlikely to be sold to other companies. Open jobs are listed, often with the due date. Outdated or closed positions are removed. On the organization's website, contact information is provided along with detailed job descriptions and necessary skills. Why apply for a position in which you are not qualified or will not be considered?

Many other sites have fees, keep your data, sell your information, or force you to click on outside links. However, many people use external websites for their search. Always check the website where you put your name and personal information first just in case. You don't want to be sorry about identity theft or a sudden bout of spam. Here are a few options that often have good internship selections.

- Ed2010.com – Fashion Journalism
- FindSpark.com
- Indeed.com
- Internship.com
- InternQueen.com
- InternMatch.com

Here is another internship opportunity. More internships are posted on our website. Note: we do not ask for or receive a fee for these. We just post internships we find.

Nordstrom – The Ambassador Program @ Nordstrom: Define the Future of Retail

> https://www.nordstrom.com/browse/theambassadorprogram
> theambassadorprogram@nordstrom.com

This internship offers high school and college students (ages 14-22) with the opportunity to share ideas and experiences while gaining mentorship in digital styling, content creation, merchandising, marketing, social media, design, technology, and retail industry business. Students will explore career interests and get advice. While this is an unpaid internship, college scholarships are available. You do not need to live near a Nordstrom, but there is a 30-minute application.

FINAL NOTE

Some students often feel they have no chance given the number of applicants and only a few openings. Competition does exist in the fashion industry. Many applicants have significant experience. Often, very talented applicants are turned down in favor of an individual who has an inside connection. Connections are often made through a college career center or a professor who knows people in the industry. Nevertheless, someone will get a position. You could be that person.

Everyone wants to work for the same major brands. However, few look for up-and-coming creators, startup companies, or smaller establishments. While you may have your heart set on your dream brand, starting small may give you valuable learning experiences. Starting at the bottom of the ladder is not a bad place. With discipline, diligence, and training, you will climb the ladder to where you envision your life.

CHAPTER 6

WHAT IS THE DIFFERENCE BETWEEN AN AA, AS, BA, BS, BFA, MFA?

"Creativity is the power to connect the seemingly unconnected."

– William Plomer

UNDERGRADUATE AND GRADUATE DEGREES

AA – Associate of Arts – 2-year degree

AS – Associate of Science – 2-year degree

BA – Bachelor of Arts – 4-year degree

BS – Bachelor of Science – 4-year degree

BFA – Bachelor of Fine Arts – 4-year degree with most classes focused on art

MFA – Master of Fine Arts – 1-2-year degree earned after the BA, BS, or BFA

Basically, BA and BS degrees are degrees that typically offer a liberal arts foundation along with a major or concentration in a specific subject. Meanwhile, a BFA is considered a professional arts-focused degree with fewer courses in English, science, math, social science, and the humanities. Thus, the BFA is a specialist qualification in the arts. A BA or BS degree in fashion design or fashion merchandising is also valuable. The BFA is more focused on the specific area of art you choose.

The BA and BS degrees include significantly more liberal arts classes and thus are more general degrees. However, the intention of the BFA degree is for students to pursue an arts-focused curriculum, and thus there are fewer general subject courses.

Finally, while many AA or AS degrees are focused on providing technical or professional skills for fashion design, an AA or AS in these areas are often interchangeable. Similarly, a BA or BS in fashion design or fashion merchandising are also relatively interchangeable. However, a BFA may be seen as different since there is typically more coursework focused on your specific pursuit, and thus, you may have more technical experiences and knowledge than someone who has a BA or BS.

AA – ASSOCIATE OF ARTS

The Associate of Arts degree is typically a 2-year general studies degree offered online or in-person by a community college. However, some universities offer AA degrees as well. The Associate of Arts degree focused on liberal arts courses often has no barrier to entry, meaning that students can enter most AA programs with a high school diploma or the equivalent. Some students take a longer or shorter time to complete the AA based upon their skills upon entering the program, certainty about the direction they are heading, and the transfer requirements for the program they desire. For example, students majoring in business may have additional business, communication, accounting, and economics requirements and need to create an academic plan early in their program to finish in two years.

AS – ASSOCIATE OF SCIENCE

The Associate of Science degree is very similar to the AA. However, the AS degree frequently emphasizes science and math and often has additional requirements.

BA – BACHELOR OF ARTS

The Bachelor of Arts degree is typically a 4-year degree offered online or in-person by a college or university. However, a few community colleges offer BA degrees as well. Some students complete their BA in fewer years depending upon AP/IB credit, dual enrollment in high school, and summer/intersession classes. Students apply to a college or university with stricter or less stringent requirements depending upon the school. The Bachelor of Arts degree frequently requires students to take lower-division (first and second year) liberal arts courses before taking specialized courses focused around a major or concentration in their third and fourth years. Some students take a longer or shorter time to complete their BA based upon their skills upon entering the program, certainty about the direction they are heading, and the chosen major. According to the National Center for Educational Statistics, college advisors aid students in finishing "on time" though less than half of all students in the United States who start a BA program do not finish their degree in four years.[1]

BS – BACHELOR OF SCIENCE

The Bachelor of Science degree is very similar to the BA. However, the BS degree frequently emphasizes science and math and often has additional requirements.

BFA – BACHELOR OF FINE ARTS

The Bachelor of Fine Arts is a 4-year college degree focusing on the arts. BFA students are often not required to take as many English, science, math, social science, and humanities courses. However, they must still complete roughly the

---

1   IEC NCES, "Digest of Education Statistics, Table 326.10," *IES NCES*, n.d., https://nces.ed.gov/programs/digest/d20/tables/dt20_326.10.asp?referer=raceindica.asp

same number of credits as a person who earns a BA or BS, and the courses are not necessarily easier. BFA students frequently take general art requirements to lay a foundation in drawing, graphic design, and courses in their specialty area during their first two years, along with basic writing and quantitative skill-building.

BFA students are traditionally art-in-practice students who learn the technical craft of their art form while putting in enormous numbers of hours practicing their skill doing assignments and participating in internships and experiential learning. Students who know that they want a future in the arts often find this avenue perfectly tailored for their pursuits. However, students who change their minds and transfer to a university in another degree program may require an additional year to make up for coursework they have not completed.

MFA – MASTER OF FINE ARTS

The Master of Fine Arts is a graduate degree for students who have completed their BA, BS, or BFA. This degree takes one to two years depending upon the program, coursework, and experiential component, which may be a capstone, practicum, internship, or thesis. While there are also MA and MS degrees, many art students who continue to earn their master's degree in the arts chose to focus on their field of interest. The MFA is an intensive immersion into a higher level of skill-building. However, students who graduate with an MFA have a broader range of talents and experiences than those who earn their bachelor's degrees. While admission into these programs is generally selective, with planning, preparation, and a good portfolio, there are options for you to pursue your interests.

THE SEVEN MAJOR DIFFERENCES BETWEEN THE ASSOCIATE, BACHELORS, AND MASTER'S DEGREES

1. Starting point
2. Academic Discipline
3. Time to Completion
4. Location of the Education
5. Educational Costs
6. Earning Power
7. Professional Opportunities

STARTING POINT

Most students who begin with an Associate of Arts (AA) or Associate of Science (AS) have no college credits. Starting from scratch with their college education, they accumulate their 60+ units beginning from this community college starting point. While most students earn AA or AS degrees at a community college, some earn this degree at a 4-year college or university.

The AA or AS is either a terminal degree, meaning that the student will not continue on with their bachelor's degree, or just a stepping stone to their BA, BS, or BFA. The difference between the associate's and bachelor's degrees is just the starting point.

The starting point for students who pursue a bachelor's degree may be farther along the traditional 4-year pathway. Meanwhile, the starting point for the master's degree (MA, MS, or MFA) begins after obtaining a bachelor's degree.

ACADEMIC DISCIPLINE

Every degree encompasses different requirements. Requirements for the AA differ from an AS. Similarly, the requirements for the BA, BS, and BFA also differ. With two additional years of coursework, the BA, BS, and BFA are more thorough. The MA, MS, and MFA build upon the bachelor's degree and dive even deeper. Fashion design students will not take the same classes as fashion merchandising, though a few may overlap. Though both are behind-the-scenes players in the fashion industry, the essential skills for each career area are distinct. Course requirements are also unique.

Furthermore, with the myriad of combinations, it is rare that any two undergraduate students have the same exact classes in the same exact order. Just as the requirements for a chemistry degree are not the same as for a biology degree, a graphic design also differs greatly from a fashion design or fashion merchandising degree. Various degrees not only include a different number of credits but different types of classes and program specifications.

TIME TO COMPLETION

Associate of Arts (AA) and Associate of Science (AS) degrees typically take two years, while most BA, BS, and BFA degrees are 4-year programs, depending upon full-time or part-time status. Students who transfer in credits or earn credits otherwise can reduce their time to completion.

Some students may choose to extend their education in fashion design or fashion merchandising by earning a second bachelor's degree in another field. By cross-training, students open more doors. For example, a degree in business on the bachelor's level or Master's in Business Administration (MBA) may lead to leadership positions.

Time in college can be reduced. Some students enter a BA, BS, or BFA program having already completed college credits because they were dual-enrolled or they took college classes directly through a college or university ahead of time. Some students have taken AP/IB tests from taking higher-level tests while in high school and earned qualifying scores to be granted credits by the college or university. Other ways students can enter at a different starting point are with credit-by-exam, CLEP tests, experiential credits, and those granted in the military.

Colleges and universities are keenly aware of the challenges students face today with work, illness, and family responsibilities. Thus, many schools of higher education offer flexible enrollment with opportunities for part-time, evening, weekend, and online classes.

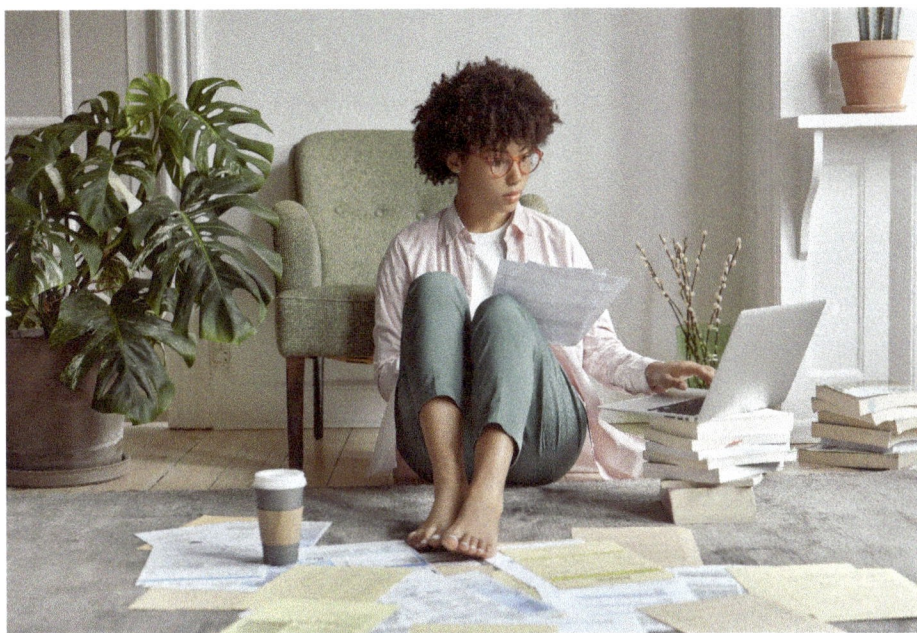

LOCATION OF THE EDUCATION

The AA and AS are earned at colleges that grant 2-year degrees. The location may be at a local community college or a university. BA, BS, and BFA programs are offered at a 4-year college or university. However, with online classes, students have the flexibility to take classes from colleges farther away as well. Thus, the location in which a typical student studies is not as set as it once was. Nevertheless, the in-person internships are often situated in corporate hubs and thus require grounding to a specific location.

EDUCATIONAL COSTS

Since the AA or AS requires a shorter amount of time and is typically completed at a lower-cost community college, the cost for an associate's degree is typically less than a bachelor's degree. Master's degree programs cost more per credit but take less time than a bachelor's degree.

On the other hand, many students can obtain financial aid in the form of grants, loans, and both merit and need-based scholarships. This aid can pay for school and reduce debt after college.

EARNING POWER

Students with more education can earn more. According to the 2019 National Center for Educational Statistics (NCES) data for the median person,[2]

Master's Degree or Higher - $70,000

Bachelor's Degree - $55,700

Associate's Degree - $43,300

High School - $35,000

PROFESSIONAL OPPORTUNITIES

Earning a BA, BS, or BFA opens more doors than an AA or AS. Similarly, an MA, MS, or MFA opens more doors than a BA, BS, or BFA. Companies typically seek employees with greater knowledge and professional experience. However, the caveat is that some companies do not want to pay more for those with more education but less experience. Training takes up much of a company's budget. There are numerous technical, software, and communication skills required when entering the professional arena. A nimble fashion designer or fashion merchandiser contributes most when they have soft skills, like creativity, collaboration, and self-motivation.

Nevertheless, the retail industry has the dual challenge of needing the manpower to design, distribute, and market apparel while also keeping the budget down so that they can afford to continue producing trending fashions. While colleges promote and develop skills and competencies, internships help cut down

---

2   IES NCES, "Annual Earnings by Educational Attainment," *IEC NCES,* May 2021, https://nces.ed.gov/programs/coe/indicator/cba

the learning curve when entering a position. This is best done by hiring those graduates who already have experience. Thus, a student with a BFA sometimes has more experience than one with a BA or BS, though plenty of students with BA and BS degrees built a portfolio of knowledge by starting early. Also, they may have a broader liberal arts sense to understand the economics, social conditions, statistical data, and psychology of changing attitudes toward fashion.

CHAPTER 7

UNIVERSITY OPTIONS: WHAT COLLEGE PROGRAMS ARE BEST FOR YOU?

"Style is the sum of so many things – beginning with a sense of who you are and having self-confidence."

– Kate Spade

There are a myriad of choices of where to focus and what colleges will satisfy your goals in the fashion industry. If you love the creative artistry of clothing choices and accessorizing, you might find interesting opportunities in the fields of fashion design, styling, packaging, or advertising. However, if you prefer the more problem-solving and analytical side of the industry, you might enjoy management or marketing. Although only 50 colleges are profiled in this book, there are many more colleges that offer similar majors. As a place to start your search, this book primarily includes four-year undergraduate college programs that are popular choices with students, though there are a few with two-year and a few graduate programs.

In choosing the right program to fit your interests, explore each college's majors, courses offered, and requirements for admission. Every school is different. I also recommend applying to ten schools so that you have choices. College profiles for fashion merchandising schools are provided in the back of this book, separated by region for your convenience. You might want to know alumni who graduated from each of the schools, internships offered, and Special Opportunities to interact with people in the industry.

Determine whether the school you are considering requires standardized tests. Some are test-optional. However, a few still require or highly recommend testing. The testing situation is fluid right now and is likely to change from year to year depending upon availability, test disruptions, and college decisions.

COLLEGE COSTS

The cost of your education may be a significant factor. Check the cost of attendance for each of the schools you are considering. However, do not let the price tag stop you from applying. First, rarely do people pay the full cost of their education. Second, more than half of all students qualify for financial aid of some sort – grants, loans, or work-study. Third, almost all colleges offer merit scholarships. These are typically based upon *talent, academics, and experience*. If you have any of these qualifications or a trifecta of all three, you may qualify for tens of thousands of dollars. Full-tuition scholarships are available as well. Many of the college's institutional scholarships are listed under the individual scholarship headings in the profile section.

COLLEGE EDUCATION OF FASHION INDUSTRY LEADERS

Here are a few individuals in the fashion industry along with the colleges they attended.

Bernard Arnault – Chairman and CEO of LVMH, Chairman of Christian Dior SE
    College: Ecole Polytechnique, France's leading engineering school

Francesca Bellettini – CEO YSL
    College: Bocconi University, Milan and University of Chicago (study abroad)

Tory Burch – Ameican Fashion Designer
    College: University of Pennsylvania in Art History

Maueen Chiquet – former CEO Chanel
    College: Yale University – BA literature with an emphasis in film

Jimmy Choo (Datuk Chow) – Malaysian Fashion Shoe Designer based in the UK
    College: Cordwainer's College, London (London College of Fashion)

Thomas Carlyle Ford – American Fashion Designer
    College: Bard College at Simon's Rock, New York University in Art History
            Parsons School of Design in Architecture

Daniel Del Core – German-Italian Fashion Designer
    College: Istituto Europeo di Design Milan

Mossimo Giannulli – American Fashion Designer
    College: Did not graduate from college

Isabelle Guichot – CEO SMCP – Board Member SMCP and Chargeurs

College: Hec Paris EESC (world-class business school)

Daphne Guinness – British Fashion Designer
    College: Did not graduate from college.

Alexandre Herchcovitch – Brazilian Fashion Designer
    College: Santa Marcelina College in Fashion

Tommy Hilfiger – American Fashion Designer
    College: Did not graduate from college

Kenneth Ize – Nigerian-Austrian Fashion Designer
    College: University of Applied Arts, Vienna

Marc Jacobs – American Fashion Designer
    College: Parsons School of Design

Betsey Johnson – American Fashion Designer
    College: Syracuse University

Donna Karan – American Fashion Designer (DKNY)
    College: Parsons School of Design

Nicholas Kirkwood – British Footwear Fashion Designer
    College: Cordwainer's College, London - (London College of Fashion)

Stella McCartney – British Fashion Designer
    College: Central Saint Martins (University of the Arts London)

Alexander McQueen - British Fashion Designer
    College: Central Saint Martins (University of the Arts London)
            Newham College (East Ham Campus)

Sandy Powell – British Costume Designer (3 Academy Awards; 15 nominations)
    College: Central School of Art and Design in Theater Design

Miuccia Prada – Italian Fashion Designer
    College: University of Milan, Ph.D. Political Science

Paula Schneider – CEO American Apparel
    College: California State University, Chico in Secondary Teaching

Maisie Schloss – American Fashion Designer of Maisie Wilen
    College: Parsons School of Design

Kate Spade – American Fashion Designer
      College: University of Kansas, Arizona State University in Journalism

Sharen Jester Turney – Former President and CEO of Victoria's Secret
      College: University of Oklahoma, B.A. in Business Education

John Varvatos – American Fashion Designer
      College: Fashion Institute of Technology
            University of Michigan, Eastern Michigan University

Charles de Vilmorin – French Fashion Designer
      College: School of the Parisian Couture Union
            French Fashion Institute

Kanye West – American Fashion Designer
      College: American Academy of Art College, Chicago State University

MANAGEMENT AND EMPLOYEE RETENTION

Skills to Know: *Management, Human Resources, Social Consciousness, Ethics*

One of the most significant challenges facing individuals during the decade from 2022 – 2032 will be locating and retaining talent. The pandemic slowed education and learning with online classes, reduced access to faculty/advising, limited access to labs, inability to attend workshops, retail closures, and fewer conferences, meetings, and shows. Health concerns rose to the top of society's importance as did financial stress, job uncertainty, and social consciousness. Many students chose to take jobs, gain work experience, or take a break from school. Some started online stores when they could not access locations for community service or continue with their sport, instrument, or hobbies. With the changes in lifestyle and fears about health, safety, and wellness, many bright and talented students developed a fearless sense of autonomy and independence, while the necessary skills ordinarily developed in school were fraught by limitations.

Finding talent within the changing hiring atmosphere will require new skills. Employees are increasingly looking elsewhere for a better opportunity. This development will require managers to earn and harness employee trust and loyalty. Top brands use the appeal of their fashions to attract new talent to their companies. However, with numerous startups and entrepreneurial thinkers eager to define their own brand, many potential job seekers are not on the market. Those who do become employed often leave to have greater autonomy.

The digital workforce has also placed demands on human resources. While many companies want their employees to work in-person, the convenience of working at home and the drudgery of commuting to work have created an environment where employees seek greater flexibility. Changes are coming. The employee talent challenge is likely to create a more global workforce where companies look for less expensive online talent from a pool of eager workers in other countries.

CYBERSECURITY

Skills to Know: *Website Development, Online Banking, Accounting, Reputation Management*

As virtual companies spring up and online forums grow, cybercriminals have used this opportunity to invade computers, terrorize individuals, and demand ransoms. Cybercrime keeps people up at night. By invading a website, cybercriminals can encrypt files on a victim's computer, locking down the site, and collecting a ransom.

Internet and computer fraud includes using the digital work spaces to execute a vindictive, malicious, or illegal attack on another computer to obtain data, damage software, or disable functions in order to obtain a financial gain. Cybercrime is somewhat different in that the reasons are not always to acquire money but could be for personal, political, social, environmental, or whimsical.

Challenges to companies – large and small – include:

- Cyber Extortion – demand for your money, belongings, or information
- Data Breach - stealing proprietary/brand information
- E-Mail Spoofing – a spamming technique to trick users into thinking a message came from an individual or company
- Forgery - the act of producing a copy of a document, signature, banknote, or other replicated item
- Information Piracy - breaking into customer accounts
- Intellectual Property Attack – Your proprietary information, recipes, formulas, codes, and methods can be stolen, sold, and reused
- Phishing – tapping on a link for a great deal, which leads a perpetrator to invade your computer, take your information, or access private information
- Predators – nefarious individuals who prey on the vulnerable for sex, drugs, or money

- Stalking – individuals who watch your actions online or in-person for a nefarious reason

Cybercrime is inconvenient, frustrating, and costly. It can ruin your reputation, deplete your bank accounts, destroy a company, and harm the personal and professional lives of your family, friends, or employees. Altogether, cybercrime wreaks havoc in victim's lives. Fixing the problem after the fact, unlocking the computer, and repairing brand damage is significantly harder and more costly than protecting a site before the crime occurs.

Our digital world leaves open the doors to voyeurs and criminals who can access your information with new and more sophisticated resources. Criminals will always exist, but you can be more aware. Protect yourself by managing your privacy, reporting cybercrime, and preventing extensive damage by responding quickly with expanded knowledge.

CHAPTER 8

COLLEGE ADMISSIONS: DEGREES, COURSEWORK, SKILLS, AND SCHOLARSHIPS

"You have to get dressed every morning, so you might as well make it fun."

– Anonymous

With notable alumni like Michael Kors, Norma Kamali, Ralph Rucci, and David Chu as well as top professors and unique courses, some consider FIT to be the leading fashion merchandising school in the country. Fashion Institute of Technology offers the following fashion design and merchandising degrees:

- BFA in Advertising and Digital Design
- AAS and BS in Advertising and Marketing Communication
- AAS in Communication Design
- BS in Cosmetics and Fragrance Marketing
- MPS in Cosmetics and Fragrance Marketing and Management
- BFA in Fabric Styling
- MA in Fashion and Textile Studies: History, Theory, Museum Practice
- BS in Fashion Business Management
- AAS, BFA, and MFA in Fashion Design
- AAS and BFA in Footwear and Accessories Design
- MPS in Global Fashion Management
- BS in International Trade and Marketing for the Fashion Industries
- AAS in Jewelry Design
- AAS in Menswear
- BFA in Packaging Design
- AAS and BS in Production Management
- BS in Production Management: Fashion and Related Industries
- BS in Technical Design
- BFA in Textile Development and Marketing
- AAS and BFA in Textile/Surface Design
- BFA Visual Presentation and Exhibition Design

Coursework includes classes like the following sample:

Fashion Management Course Options	Fashion Design Course Options
Sustainability in Fashion Merchandising	20th Century Style for the 21st Century Aesthetic
Corporate Social Responsibility	CAD for Fashion Design and Development
Data Insights and Fashion Analytics	Advanced Digital Fashion Design
Leadership Development for Retailing	Accessories that have Changed Fashion
Global Merchandising	Haute Couture Embellishments
Merchandising Strategies	Designer Sportswear Incubator

SCHOLARSHIPS

Nearly every school in the United States offers need-based scholarships. However, most schools offer merit scholarships. Many are listed in the profile section. Check it out.

Below are a couple of schools chosen at random to give you a sense of a few of the options listed in the profile section.

Marist College

- BS in Fashion Merchandising

The Silver Needle Runway is the largest of Marist College's events, held since 1984. Continually growing, this student-produced showcase highlights student designers and their works, with approximately 2000 people in attendance. A presentation of awards and scholarships follows the runway show. Awards have been provided by Kate Spade, MPorium, Cutty Sark, and Young Menswear Association, among others.

Columbia College Chicago

- BA in Fashion Studies, with concentrations in Merchandising and Product Development

Applicants, including international students, are automatically considered for talent-based scholarships. A digital portfolio or audition is required. Numerous awards are offered.

Iowa State University

- BS in Apparel, Merchandising, & Design

Iowa State offers merit-based awards to students of any major. These awards are based on GPA and ACT/SAT.

Savannah College of Art and Design (SCAD)

- BFA in Fashion Marketing and Management

SCAD also offers two full-tuition scholarships: The May and Paul Poetter Scholarship and the Frances Larkin McCommon Scholarship. These two scholarships are based on superior academic and/or artistic achievement.

The Fields Family Prestige Scholarship and Jacques Weber International Scholarship offer fashion and textile students varying award amounts.

Southern Methodist University

- BA in Fashion Media

SMU offers several scholarship opportunities to students, including the President's Scholar Award (full tuition and fees for up to 8 semesters), the SMU Distinguished Scholarship (maximum $25,000 per year for four years), and the Second Century Scholars ($20,000 per year for four years), among many others. *SMU does not have a degree in fashion merchandising, only fashion media.*

COLLEGE ADMISSIONS:

Success in the Face of Uncertainty

There are no guarantees in college admissions. However, planning is essential for success. The most beneficial advice is to pursue your passions with gusto, train to be the best you can be, take advantage of internships and experiences, and meet lots of people along the way. Remember, "life is a journey, not a destination." Often the journey is more exciting, leading to lessons, friendships, and indelible moments. However, the fact is…in the end, if college is your goal, then there are a few things you need to know to be successful.

Should you worry about grades? Of course. You should also take classes that will challenge you. Colleges pick the best candidates from those who apply. Students must be academically prepared, socially conscious, and talented in a few different areas in which they are passionate (conceptual design, graphic arts, costumes, theater, acting, singing, dance, musical instruments, debate, public speaking, leadership, athletics, community service, computer coding, robotics, construction, etc.).

The selection process is not much different than companies picking the most talented and collaborative employees. While colleges are more or less competitive, companies may have only one job and fifty resumes. Discover your unique drive and internal motivations. Be exceptional at what you choose to do academically, personally, and professionally.

Most of all,

You Do You!

TALENT FOCUSED

Not all schools require high grades and test scores. Many are simply interested in selecting students who are the most talented, most driven, and the most willing to be team players on the college campus. Thus, while you should take a solid set of courses and fulfill requirements, only the top schools emphasize completing a challenging curriculum, high grades, and standardized test scores.

FOR HIGHLY SELECTIVE COLLEGES, TALENT IS JUST THE BEGINNING

A few highly selective colleges seek extraordinary talent over academics, but most zero in on a student's challenging courses and high grades. To gain admission into the most highly selective colleges, you must take the most challenging course load you can manage and succeed. Highly selective colleges want disciplined, brilliant scholars AND remarkably creative students.

Determine what you can handle, knowing that some colleges with extremely competitive admission will only take students who have completed more than ten AP, IB, or honors classes over the four years, including AP Calculus. Note that AP Statistics is not of equal rigor in their eyes. Why, then, would these most competitive colleges require a difficult problem-solving class that is beyond the scope of what you need for your major? This situation is the $50,000 question. However, if this requirement seems daunting, remember that most colleges accepting students for artistic fields do not need these types of classes.

College admissions can feel like a rollercoaster of energy and emotion. Creating a portfolio of talent, training, and experience is just the beginning. Meanwhile, some colleges want to see standardized test scores. Applications and essays may seem easy at first, but managing the various requirements and deadlines can be difficult. Therefore, this application period is a good time to get a calendar and organize your tasks.

STANDARDIZED TESTING

A few schools require testing. Check first. Many colleges are test optional. This means that you are not required to take the SAT or ACT. However, if you do have a good score, it may make all the difference in accepting you. College admissions offices are studying this topic and considering their future policies. Much of their concern began with cancelations worldwide due to the pandemic. Schools did not want to let students into their site who may be infected. In addition, social distancing limited the number of students who could take a test at a site at a time.

Yet, college admissions decisions were once centered around grades and test scores. The change has rattled admissions departments. Meanwhile, colleges proclaim that test-optional truly means that the test is not required, but evidence proves otherwise. Thus, many students are still taking the test and working around the hurdles amid all of the confusion. Competition continues to drive students to present evidence to show that they are worthy candidates.

In the end, colleges need to make a final decision between very good candidates. If one student has a high score, that student may have a higher likelihood of admission depending upon the admissions committee's decision-making process. Data show that students who submitted scores within the college's range or higher were accepted at a higher rate than those without a score. Some schools are test blind. These colleges say that they do not consider your scores. A few of these colleges still provide a place for you to input your scores. Thus, they are not truly blind. Nevertheless, this decision is yours. If the school does not require an admissions test, then you can choose to take the test. If your academics are solid and you are willing to prepare, you should take the test.

APPLYING EARLY

Early Action (EA), Restricted Early Action (REA), and Early Decision (ED)

With low acceptance rates, the chance to get more scholarship money, and chaos surrounding the cancellations and changes in AP, IB, SAT, and ACT testing, students clamor to apply early to schools. In addition, applications to top schools increased during the pandemic, resulting in colleges making difficult admissions decisions in their quest to build a diverse, talented, and engaged class of students. Furthermore, students applying early have access to many more scholarship options. This confluence sent students in droves to apply early and this trend is likely to continue.

In Early Action (EA), Restricted Early Action (REA), and Early Decision (ED), students apply in late summer or early fall to college and generally find out around winter break, though some decisions come out earlier and a few arrive later. This advantage not only includes students the chance for more scholarship money in some cases but the benefit of finding out early reduces the tension of the long waiting period to find out about Regular Decision schools.

Early Action (EA) and Restricted Early Action (REA) are different. In restricted early action, a limitation is placed on either how many or what colleges you can apply to simultaneously. Many REA schools do not allow students to apply to other early action schools, though some will allow students to apply EA to public colleges. In addition, some schools like Georgetown will allow students to apply EA elsewhere but not apply to a binding Early Decision (ED) program where the student commits to attending if they are accepted. However, most EA schools do not have these restrictions, and some students apply to a handful of EA schools during the admissions process.

Early Decision (ED) is a binding agreement between the student and college with signatures from the student's parents and the high school. Each of these parties acknowledges and agrees that, if granted admission, they will attend. There are incentives. Frequently, acceptance rates are higher with ED. Also, at some schools, a large percentage of their class is filled with students who profess their unequivocal love for their dream school. Students who know they have a top choice school, have the necessary admissions requirements, and are committed to accepting the binding agreement to attend, should apply ED.

COMMON APPLICATION, COALITION APPLICATION, OR COLLEGE-SPECIFIC APPLICATION

Every college's process is unique. However, there are a few commonalities. In 2022, approximately 900 colleges used the Common App; about 150 colleges used the Coalition Application. A few used both. The University of California system has its own application as do the California State Universities and the Texas schools. The Common App and Coalition App may be started early. In your junior year, consider getting a head start on reviewing what is required. The college-specific questions may change each year. However, the basic application is generally the same and can be created ahead of time. At the end of July, make a copy of everything you have completed just in case.

In August, most admissions applications are open and ready for you to dive into the college-specific questions. Some schools admit on a rolling basis. 'Rolling' means that periodically, after all of the materials are received, the admissions committee determines who they will accept, and they send the notification right away. Many students are accepted as early as August. The thrill of acceptance cannot be overstated.

Complete the application fully. Think carefully about optional sections. Typically, they offer you the chance to provide the school with just the right cherry on top of the ice cream sundae. If you have absolutely nothing to say, then leave it blank. There are often required essays on the main Common App and the supplemental applications for each school. Some include scholarship essays. Start early.

DECISIONS, DECISIONS: WAITING FOR A RESPONSE

The period between submitting your application and getting your results may not require a tremendous amount of work, but it does require patience and diligence. First, most schools will send you a link to a portal where you will check your results, though the most important reason for checking every couple of weeks is to ensure that they are not missing something or have not offered you the chance to apply for an extra scholarship. Check your portal regularly. Otherwise, read the correspondence that the school may send through your e-mail.

Waiting is difficult. This is a tough period because students want to know. However, on the portal, the college typically lists the date they will send out the results. You will find out soon.

CELEBRATING ACCEPTANCES AND DEALING WITH REJECTION

Acceptance is not guaranteed. The probabilities are low at the most highly selective schools. However, you just need to work to have what it takes and give this commitment all you have.

Fashion Merchandising - Top 10 Most Competitive Schools by Admit Rate

1. Cornell University - 11%
2. Florida State University - 32%
3. University of Texas, Austin (UT Austin) - 32%
4. Fashion Institute of Design and Merchandising (FIDM) - 39%

5. California State University, Long Beach (CSULB) - 42%

6. North Carolina State University, Raleigh College of Design - 46%

7. University of Georgia - 48%

8. Southern Methodist University (SMU) - 53%

9. Marist College - 55%

10. Fashion Institute of Technology (FIT) - 59%

When you find out the results, you will celebrate your acceptances. Congratulations! These go on your list of wins. Check your financial aid and scholarship package. Money is often an important factor in making your decision. Consider visiting the school. Many students apply by only looking at pictures and profiles on a website or book. There is nothing that replaces the actual visit. After all, you will be spending a few years there.

However, you may not be accepted everywhere, and you apply. The pandemic's uncertainty added more question marks to an already complicated set of admissions processes. The 2020 buzzword was *resilience*. It is never easy to be rejected. However, rejection happens, and you will survive this. Note that many colleges still accept applications in April, May, and June. Look up those colleges if you did not get accepted or if you want to see what other schools might be good options for you. You will be surprised to see the colleges on the list.

WAITLISTS: THE ART OF WAITING

Confirm immediately if you are given a waitlist spot and still want to attend. There is often a deadline. You do not want to miss this date. If you are no longer interested or have selected another school, go into the portal and turn down the offer. Someone else is bound to be thrilled by your anonymous gift.

Next, if you are highly interested, find the location on the portal or site designated by the college to update them on what you have done – accomplishments, awards, extra class, honors, art, shows, or films. You only want to add what they have not yet seen, but if you have taken the initiative to do something more than what you originally stated on the application, by all means, tell them. You could just wait for their decision, but you are better off being proactive and showing that you really want to be at their school.

A few students do get off of the waitlists at most schools. Meanwhile, you will have to deposit somewhere else before the May 1st deadline. Stay hopeful. This next year will be a significant step along your journey. Relax!

DETERMINING FINANCIAL AID

You do not need to complete the FAFSA (Free Application for Federal Student Aid) or CSS Profile (College Scholarship Service) if you do not need aid. However, a handful of schools want to see one or both of these forms to obtain scholarships. Check now since there are deadlines.

If you completed the FAFSA (and CSS profile, if required), the financial aid package you receive would be viewable on your portal. The college will delineate the amounts you will receive for grants, loans, and work-study. Some students turn down work-study, but I caution against that. There are jobs on campus where you conduct research, work with a professor, work in the library, or assist an athletic team. Some of these jobs pay well, and you might have even done them as a volunteer.

If your financial situation changed since applied, you may be able to renegotiate the amount they offered.

CHOOSING THE RIGHT SCHOOL FOR YOU

With the turmoil of the pandemic, disruption in clubs, sports, and experiential activities, and serious family health concerns, access to some opportunities has been non-existent. Most training and practice have been virtual. Furthermore, few students have traveled to visit colleges due to the crisis. However, with college costs for four years around $300,000 at some schools, college is the most significant investment some families will ever make. Furthermore, student loans can saddle a student in debt for a decade or more.

Financial decisions are key. However, there are many variables in deciding which school to choose. Will I be able to afford my education? Will classes be online or in-person? Will I be able to continue my training? Will I get to visit the colleges first? Can I live through the repercussions of stressful decision-making? Should I defer my admissions and take a year off?

Once you receive your acceptances, you need to make a decision. Focus on your future. What is trending? What do people want? How can you deliver?

You've Got This!

CHAPTER 9

POST-PANDEMIC EMPLOYMENT OUTLOOK: STATISTICS AND ECONOMIC PROJECTIONS

"The door of opportunity will open only when you decide to step outside the door of your comfort zone."

– Kylie Francis

ECONOMIC OUTLOOK IN THE FASHION DESIGN AND FASHION MERCHANDISING INDUSTRIES

Fashion merchandising attracts thousands of students each year to pursue a career in the business side of fashion. There are numerous directions to go with fashion merchandising. Since this career focuses on the business side of fashion, fashion merchandisers must improve the bottom line of companies. Fashion merchandisers with solid business skills tend to make more money than fashion designers.

Working on the coordination, organization, forecasts, display concept, sales, production, and distribution sides of the business, decision-making skills are critical. A mistake can cost millions of dollars. Positioning products for maximum customer visibility can be extraordinarily exhilarating. Fashion shows, creative styling, photography, videography, social media, and website visibility are attractive to the go-getter student.

The economic outlook for retail stores does not look good in the near term, but this will change with post-pandemic societal changes. Forecasters believe retail will pick up. For now, explore e-commerce. What attracts you to these sites? What are brick-and-mortar stores doing to get your business? Notice the changes in window displays, mannequins, styling, and sales racks.

Management requires attention to detail and a recognition of the needs and wants of its customers. Managers are paid better because they are held accountable for a store's success. Retail managers are responsible for training staff. How attentive are they to your needs? Consumer demands continue to change. Which companies are adapting well to these changes? If this direction is interesting to you, then you should make sure that the education you receive includes business management classes.

Whether you desire a more creative role or a more business-oriented focus, there is a place for you. However, there are typically more applicants than positions. With the volume of people choosing this direction, top jobs tend to go to those with more education and experience. Also, the more competitive markets require additional skills, education, and ambition.

Do not let the number of people applying for undergraduate or graduate degree programs or an internship/job stop you. If this is the field you want to pursue, pave the road in front of you and drive. An internship or two would not hurt you in your pursuit. Although most internships are unpaid, you will find that most applicants will have one or more.

If you are serious, you can make a fantastic career out of your pursuit. Initiative-taking persistence, talent, creativity, and moxie can get you into your desired college program and career. You may have to start at the very bottom of the ladder, but you can climb the rungs methodically one by one.

Companies want to know the work ethic, personality, and professionalism of the employees they choose. An internship allows you to get to know their corporate climate better and allows them to get to know you better too. Thus, many companies hire the interns they already know and feel are the best fit for their environment and who might work for them in the long run. Even so, some still choose candidates from the piles of resumes and cover letters that have been submitted.

Education unlocks doors. In fashion merchandising, this is particularly true. Management, statistics, marketing, finance, accounting, and business communication are invaluable tools in this career pursuit. Your education, highlighted on your resume, can move your application to the top of the pile.

FASHION DESIGN ECONOMIC OUTLOOK

Bureau of Labor Statistics - Fashion Designers

2020 Median Pay: $75,810 per year
Bachelor's Degree: Fashion Design or Fashion Merchandising
Number of Jobs in 2020: 27,800
Job Growth: No change
Location of Most Positions: New York and California

Fashion designers design and create clothing, accessories, and footwear. The work environment is predominantly in wholesale or manufacturing establishments, apparel companies, retailers, theater, dance companies, and design firms. The work is both creative on the design side and technical on the production side.

TECH DESIGNERS VS CREATIVE DESIGNERS

Do you like to sketch, illustrate, and do graphic design? You might love the creative design route. You can draw on paper or use programs like Adobe Illustrator. You get to imagine and create fashionable garments, choose fabrics and add trims and adornments, enhance whatever you envision.

Technical designers though, are less focused on inventing ideas and more honed in on apparel production. What instructions are necessary to create a particular garment? This detailed work includes providing clarity regarding patterns, notions, sewing, fit, and packaging. Technical designers are often called the engineers behind the garments. With fittings, alterations, and changes in the specifications, communication between the creative and technical teams is essential.

From concept (creative designer) to product specifications (technical designer) there are numerous steps to ensure that the garment makes sense.

POSSIBLE CAREER OPTIONS

Account Executive

Art Director

Beauty, Makeup, or Perfume Executive

Brand Manager

Consumer Behavior Analyst

Costume Designer

Creative Director

Design Director

E-Commerce Manager

Fabric and Apparel Patternmakers

Fashion Analyst

Fashion Designer

Fashion Editor-in-Chief

Fashion Forecaster

Fashion Freelance Writer

Fashion Merchandiser

Fashion or Textile Buyer

Fashion Photographer

Fashion Publisher

Fashion Show Producer

Fashion Sustainability Executive

Hand and Machine Sewers

Marketing Director

Marketing Manager

Pressers Textile

Product Developer

Product Lifestyle Manager

Public Relations Manager

Retail Management

Sourcing Manager

Stylist

Tailors, Dressmakers, and Custom Sewers

Textile Bleaching and Dyeing

Textile Winding, Twisting, Drawing Machine Setters, Operators, and Tenders

Textile Knitting and Weaving

Textile, Apparel, and Furnishing Workers

Whatever direction you pursue, if you lay a foundation, undaunted by the competition, and are unafraid of starting at the bottom, you will do fine. Hard work and creativity go a long way in this industry. Start by getting a solid education.

CHAPTER 10

NEXT STEPS: PREPARATION AND REAL-WORLD SKILLS

"If you obey all the rules, you miss all the fun."

– Katherine Hepburn

BOLD NETWORKING

Networking takes social skills and a bit of moxie. From elevator speeches and restaurant encounters to tradeshows and industry meetings, your job is to find a way to get in front of people. How can you be recognized? Meet people and hand out your resume. Give them your business card and ask for their business card. Then, follow up and ask if you can call or meet them for lunch or coffee, even if asking may seem uncomfortable. Stay in touch with the people you meet, even if you just meet them out of happenstance or serendipity. Keep a log with each person's phone, e-mail, identifying information, and both date and location where you met. You never know when you will need it.

STAY IN TOUCH

Be proactive but professional. There is a delicate balance between keeping in touch and obsessively contacting an individual. Since each minute is critical to busy decision-makers, constant communication can overwhelm and frustrate the person you are attempting to impress or influence. Staying in touch every couple of months is fine. However, communicating more frequently can be overpowering. Remember that life is long. In the fashion industry, the network you grow will be valuable throughout your career.

Befriend other go-getters. They may be tremendous allies in the future, even if you are presently seeking the same position. Fellow interns today are likely to be very successful and hold prominent positions in the future. While staying in touch with "important" people may prove helpful now, remaining connected with your peers, particularly those who are bright and creative, may lead to mutually beneficial partnerships later. Thus, your contemporaries or peers are influential people…although not yet.

After interviewing at a few places, you may choose a position elsewhere. Even so, do not lose touch with the people you meet or burn bridges along the way.

This industry is not that big, and you will continually see movers and shakers on all levels of the fashion world. You never know. They may contact you to collaborate one day or meet for coffee at an event. Networking is a two-way street, and the best networkers know this.

COLLEGE AND CAREER CENTERS

Almost every college has a career center. There may be a specific career liaison in the fashion, fashion design, merchandising, business, or art department. Contact them for help in your search process. Not only can they assist with resume and cover letter services, but they may have contacts in the industry. Past graduates who are in the fashion industry make great connections. They have been through the ropes, they know a few people, and they might be able to get you an interview or into a fashion industry event. Any contact may be able to get your foot into the door.

LINKEDIN

LinkedIn is especially helpful for career searches. You can find numerous influential contacts on LinkedIn. After each interview, connect with them on LinkedIn. Keep a contact list of individuals you know in the fashion industry. Do not constantly try to connect with people you do not really know. However, if you have made the connection, occasionally keep in touch.

While some LinkedIn message boxes may be full and you may not get a reply, you can try. Occasionally, you hit on a lucky break. Though I do not have time to communicate with everyone, I have connected with some of my most inspiring authors, advisors, and intellectual leaders through LinkedIn.

FINALLY

Most people are willing to help you. Five percent will not. Thus, you have a 19 out of 20 chance of interacting with decent people who have the time and will give you advice. Don't lose faith in humanity just because you ran into a few people who are too busy to stop for you or are too self-absorbed that they cannot answer your question.

- Work ethic is everything.
- Excellence is expected.
- Learn what you do not know on your own time.
- Come to work prepared.
- Take constructive criticism well.
- Keep your cool under pressure.
- Avoid being timid.
- Stay on task.
- Come early.
- Stay late.
- Take your work seriously.
- Do more than expected.
- Read your e-mail/texts after hours in case something is important.
- Ask questions. No question is too stupid.
- Maintain a clean workspace.
- Dress and act professionally.
- Don't gossip or complain.
- Avoid frustrating your phenomenally busy supervisor.
- Be straightforward, and don't beat around the bush.

You've Got This!

4
Regions

50
Programs

COLLEGE
PROFILES AND
REQUIREMENTS

WEST

MIDWEST

NORTHEAST

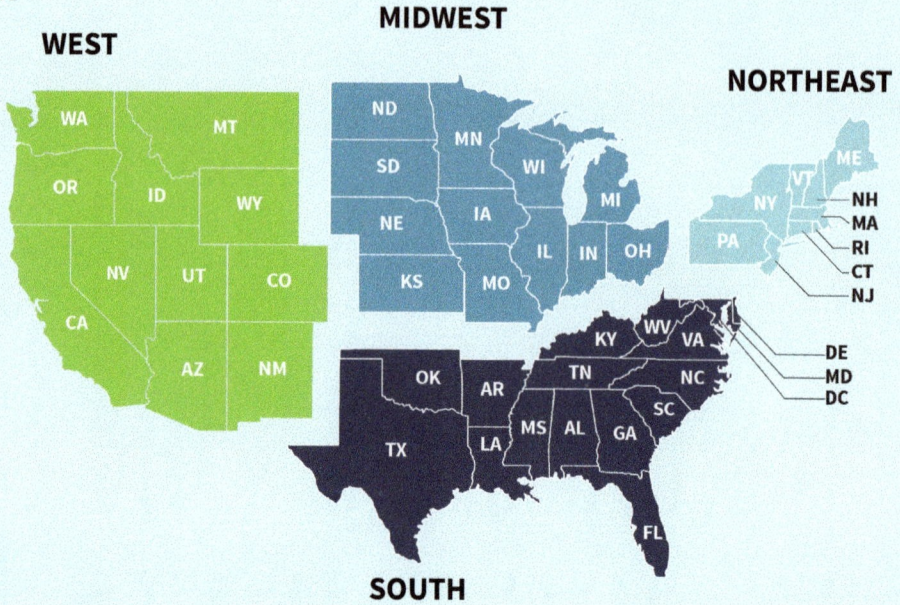

SOUTH

PROGRAMS BY REGION
U.S. CENSUS BUREAU CLASSIFICATIONS

REGION 1 – NORTHEAST

Connecticut, Maine, Massachusetts, New Hampshire, New Jersey, New York, Pennsylvania, Rhode Island, and Vermont

REGION 2 – MIDWEST

Illinois, Indiana, Iowa, Kansas, Michigan, Minnesota, Missouri, Nebraska, North Dakota, Ohio, South Dakota, and Wisconsin

REGION 3 – SOUTH

Alabama, Arkansas, Delaware, District of Columbia, Florida, Georgia, Kentucky, Louisiana, Maryland, Mississippi, North Carolina, Oklahoma, South Carolina, Tennessee, Texas, Virginia, and West Virginia

REGION 4 – WEST

Alaska, Arizona, California, Colorado, Hawaii, Idaho, Montana, Nevada, New Mexico, Oregon, Utah, Washington, and Wyoming

LIST OF FASHION MERCHANDISING PROGRAMS

The programs listed in the following pages include top fashion merchandising programs. In addition, this book also lists the top fashion design, costume design, and fashion photography programs. Many students interested in fashion are often also interested in the artistic side of clothing design, presentation, and marketing. There are many facets of the fashion/clothing design world. One of these other areas might be a good option for you.

Fashion merchandising is not for everyone. Although immensely rewarding, there are challenges. You might choose an alternative path somewhere down the road.

Thus, this book aims to provide you with a more comprehensive set of lists so that you can explore your options. Keep the book handy. Even after you begin college, you may find the additional programs in the back are helpful for connections or summer programs.

Creating lists is often tedious and cumbersome. These lists were gathered to help you with this task.

Descriptions of the college programs, tuition, requirements, and deadlines are accurate as of December 2021. The requirements may have changed somewhat by the time you purchase this book, but this information is a great place to start!

Note: To simplify the text and fit information into the charts and descriptions, abbreviations were used as well as shortened sentences and acronyms.

CONNECTICUT

MAINE

MASSACHUSETTS

NEW HAMPSHIRE

NEW JERSEY

NEW YORK

PENNSYLVANIA

RHODE ISLAND

VERMONT

CHAPTER 11

CHAPTER 11

REGION ONE

NORTHEAST

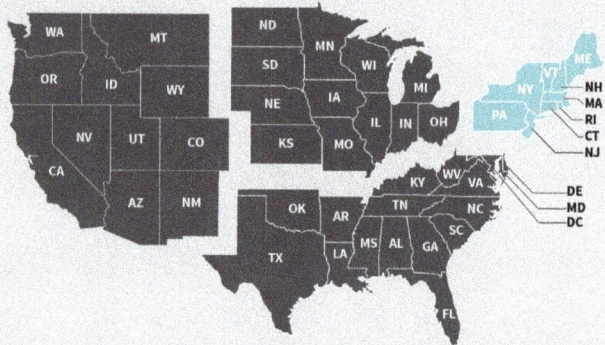

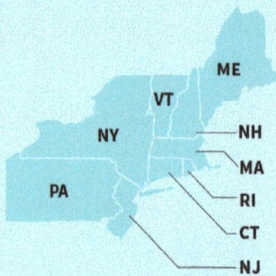

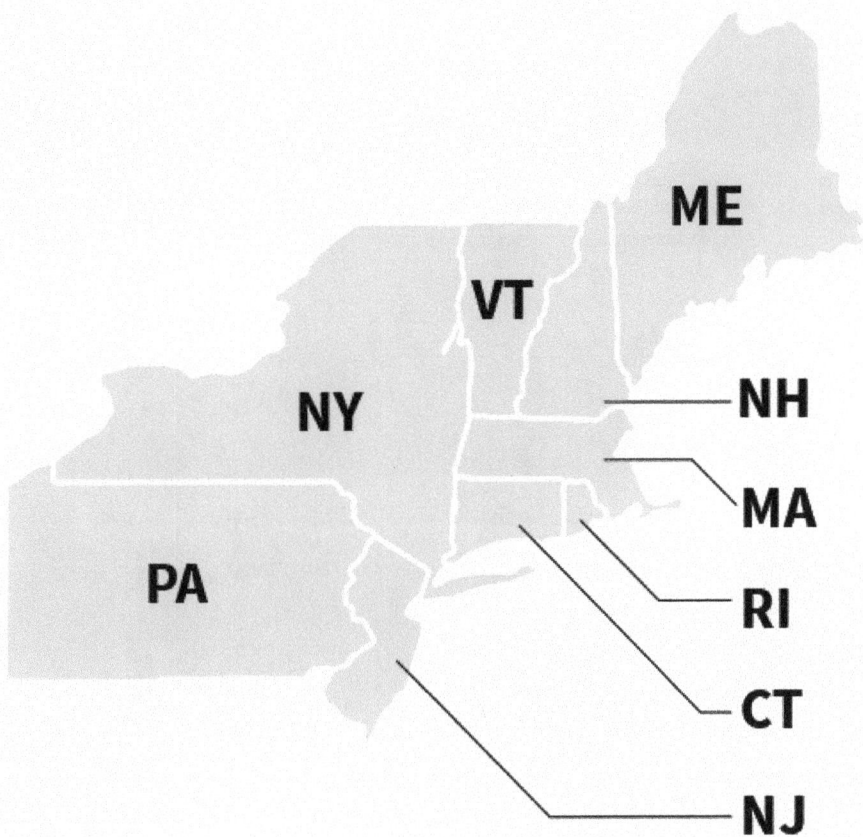

8 Programs | 9 States

1. NY – Cornell University
2. NY – Fashion Institute of Technology (FIT)
3. NY – LIM College
4. NY – Marist College
5. NY – Parsons - The New School
6. PA - Drexel University
7. PA - Thomas Jefferson University
8. RI - University of Rhode Island

FASHION MERCHANDISING PROGRAMS

School	Avg. GPA, SAT Evidence-Based Reading Writing (ERW), SAT Math (M), and ACT Composite (C) Early Decision (ED): Yes/No	Admission Statistics	Program(s)	Portfolio and/ or Interview Required (Req.)
Cornell University 430 College Ave., Ithaca, NY 14850	GPA: N/A SAT (ERW): 680-750 SAT (M): 720-790 ACT (C): 32-35 ED: No	Admit Rate: 11% Undergrad Enrollment: 14,743 Total Enrollment: 23,620	BS in Fashion Design & Management, Option in Fashion Design Management Degrees Awarded in the Program(s) (2020): N/A	Portfolio: Req. Interview: Not req.
Fashion Institute of Technology (FIT) 227 West 27th Street, New York City, NY 10001	GPA: N/A SAT (ERW): N/A SAT (M): N/A ACT (C): N/A *FIT is test optional. ED: No	Admit Rate: 59% Undergrad Enrollment: 7,959 Total Enrollment: 8,191	BS in Fashion Business Management BS in International Trade and Marketing for the Fashion Industries BS in Production Management: Fashion and Related Industries BFA in Textile Development and Marketing Degrees Awarded in the Program(s) (2020): 408	Portfolio: Not req. Interview: Not req.

School	Avg. GPA, SAT Evidence-Based Reading Writing (ERW), SAT Math (M), and ACT Composite (C) Early Decision (ED): Yes/No	Admission Statistics	Program(s)	Portfolio and/or Interview Required (Req.)
LIM College 216 E 45th St, New York, NY 10017	GPA: N/A SAT (ERW): N/A SAT (M): N/A ACT (C): N/A *LIM College is test optional. ED: No	Admit Rate: 84% Undergrad Enrollment: 1,349 Total Enrollment: 1,681	BBA in Business of Fashion BS in Fashion Media BBA in Fashion Merchandising BPS in Fashion Merchandising Degrees Awarded in the Program(s) (2020): 191	Portfolio: Not req. Interview: May be required
Marist College 3399 North Road, Poughkeepsie, NY 12601	GPA: 3.4 SAT (ERW): 580-660 SAT (M): 560-660 ACT (C): 26-31 *Marist College is test optional. ED: No	Admit Rate: 55% Undergrad Enrollment: 5,682 Total Enrollment: 6,600	BS in Fashion Merchandising, concentrations: Business Fashion Promotion Product Development Degrees Awarded in the Program(s) (2020): 96	Portfolio: Not req. Interview: Not req.
Parsons - The New School 66 Fifth Avenue, New York, NY 10011	GPA: N/A SAT (ERW): 580-680 SAT (M): 560-680 ACT (C): 26-30 ED: No	Admit Rate: 69% Undergrad Enrollment: 6,399 Total Enrollment: 9,047	AAS Fashion Marketing and Communication Degrees Awarded in the Program(s) (2020): 60	Portfolio: Not req. Interview: Not req.

NORTHEAST

FASHION MERCHANDISING PROGRAMS

School	Avg. GPA, SAT Evidence-Based Reading Writing (ERW), SAT Math (M), and ACT Composite (C) Early Decision (ED): Yes/No	Admission Statistics	Program(s)	Portfolio and/or Interview Required (Req.)
Drexel University 3250 Chestnut Street, MacAlister Hall, Suite 4020, Philadelphia, PA 19104	GPA: N/A SAT (ERW): 590-680 SAT (M): 590-700 ACT (C): 25-31 ED: No	Admit Rate: 77% Undergrad Enrollment: 14,616 Total Enrollment: 23,589	BS in Design & Merchandising Degrees Awarded in the Program(s) (2020): N/A	Portfolio: Not req. Interview: Not req.
Thomas Jefferson University 4201 Henry Avenue, Philadelphia, PA 19144	GPA: N/A SAT (ERW): 550-630 SAT (M): 540-640 ACT (C): 20-27 ED: No	Admit Rate: 70% Undergrad Enrollment: 3,783 Total Enrollment: 8,286	BS in Fashion Merchandising & Management Degrees Awarded in the Program(s) (2020): 68	Portfolio: Not req. but optional for all majors Interview: Not req.
University of Rhode Island 35 Campus Avenue, Kingston, Rhode Island 02881	GPA: 3.56 SAT (ERW): 550-630 SAT (M): 540-630 ACT (C): 23-28 ED: No	Admit Rate: 76% Undergrad Enrollment: 14,904 Total Enrollment: 17,649	BS in Textiles, Fashion Merchandising, and Design, concentrations: Fashion Merchandising Apparel Design Textile Science BS in Textile Marketing Degrees Awarded in the Program(s) (2020): 13	Portfolio: Not req. Interview: Not req.

100%
Cotton

CORNELL UNIVERSITY

Address: 430 College Ave., Ithaca, NY 14850
Website: https://www.human.cornell.edu/hcd/academics/
undergraduate-study/fashion-design-and-management
Contact: https://www.human.cornell.edu/contact
Request for Information: https://admissions.cornell.edu/
requesting-information
Phone: (607) 254-2700
Email: admissions@cornell.edu

COST OF ATTENDANCE:

*In-State Tuition & Fees: $40,382 | **Additional Expenses:** $20,001
Total: $60,383

Out-of-State Tuition & Fees: $60,286 | **Additional Expenses:** $20,001
Total: $80,287

*Note: The College of Human Ecology is a State Contract College, therefore there is an in-state tuition rate.

Financial Aid: https://finaid.cornell.edu/

ADDITIONAL INFORMATION:

Available Degree(s)
- BS in Fashion Design & Management, Option in Fashion Design Management

Freshman Portfolio Requirement
- Submit via SlideRoom
- Written Statements
  - 3 responses, 250-word, 250-word, and 500-word
- Case Study
  - Follow prompt (9 pages maximum)
  - Create new fashion brand or reinvent an existing brand and discuss (1) brand name selection, (2) customer lifestyle images, (3) customer looks, and (4) brand promotion
- Optional creative work (max 3 additional images), such as photos, videos, blog posts, or garments

For more information, visit: https://www.human.cornell.edu/
admissions/undergraduate/fashioncasestudy

Scholarships Offered
Cornell does not offer any merit aid or athletic scholarships. All aid is need-based. According to Cornell, "there is no standard 'income bracket' or cut-off for grant aid recipients; eligibility is determined on a case-by-case basis." Students are also automatically considered for endowed scholarships when they apply for financial aid. For more information, visit: https://finaid.cornell.edu/types-aid/
grants-and-scholarships

Special Opportunities
Students may be enrolled in the Fashion Science and Apparel Design (FSAD) Honors Program. For more information, visit: https://www.
human.cornell.edu/fsad/academics/undergraduate/honors

Notable Alumni
- Gizelle Begler: International Fashion Designer

CONNECTICUT

MAINE

MASSACHUSETTS

NEW HAMPSHIRE

NEW JERSEY

NEW YORK

PENNSYLVANIA

RHODE ISLAND

VERMONT

FASHION INSTITUTE OF TECHNOLOGY (FIT)

Address: 227 West 27th Street, New York City, NY 10001
Website: https://www.fitnyc.edu/admissions/programs/index.php
Contact: http://www.fitnyc.edu/about/contact/index.php
Request for Information: http://www.fitnyc.edu/admissions/request-information.php
Phone: (212) 217-3760
Email: fitinfo@fitnyc.edu

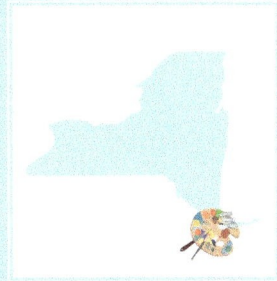

COST OF ATTENDANCE:

In-State Tuition & Fees: $7,920 | **Additional Expenses:** $18,556
Total: $26,476

Out-of-State Tuition & Fees: $22,242 | **Additional Expenses:** $18,556
Total: $40,798

Financial Aid: https://www.fitnyc.edu/admissions/costs/financial-aid/index.php

ADDITIONAL INFORMATION:

Available Degree(s)

High school students must first apply to the AAS program. Suggested AAS degrees for the BS programs are as follow:

- BS in Fashion Business Management
  - AAS Fashion Business Management
- BS in International Trade and Marketing for the Fashion Industries
  - Flexible, but AAS Advertising and Marketing Communications is recommended
- BS in Production Management: Fashion and Related Industries
  - AAS Production Management: Fashion and Related Industries
- BS in Textile Development and Marketing
  - AAS Textile Development and Marketing

All the AAS degrees fall under FIT's School of Business and Technology. There is no portfolio requirement.

Scholarships Offered

FIT scholarships are donor scholarships typically gifted to students with high financial need. The average award is $1,100. For more information, visit: https://www.fitnyc.edu/admissions/costs/financial-aid/scholarships/index.php

Special Opportunities

Students in the Fashion Business Management BS program may study in Florence, Italy during their entire 3rd year or 5th or 6th semester. For more information, visit: http://www.fitnyc.edu/study-abroad/programs/fit-in-italy/index.php

Notable Alumni

- Fran Boller: Executive Vice President at Nike
- Calvin Klein: Founder of Calvin Klein, Inc.
- Michael Kors: Chief Creative Officer and Honorary Chairman at Michael Kors

CONNECTICUT

MAINE

MASSACHUSETTS

NEW HAMPSHIRE

NEW JERSEY

NEW YORK

PENNSYLVANIA

RHODE ISLAND

VERMONT

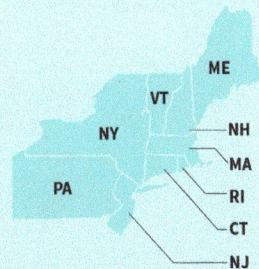

NORTHEAST

CONNECTICUT

MAINE

MASSACHUSETTS

NEW HAMPSHIRE

NEW JERSEY

NEW YORK

PENNSYLVANIA

RHODE ISLAND

VERMONT

LIM COLLEGE

Address: 216 E 45th St, New York, NY 10017
Website: https://www.limcollege.edu/academics/degrees
Contact: https://www.limcollege.edu/contact-us
Request for Information: https://admissions.limcollege.edu/register/requestinfo
Phone: (212) 752-1530
Email: admissions@limcollege.edu

COST OF ATTENDANCE:

Tuition & Fees: $27,030 | **Additional Expenses:** $23,950
Total: $50,980

Financial Aid: https://www.limcollege.edu/admissions/financial-aid-options

ADDITIONAL INFORMATION:

Available Degree(s)

- BBA in Business of Fashion
- BS in Fashion Media
- BBA in Fashion Merchandising
- BPS in Fashion Merchandising

Freshman Portfolio Requirement

There is no portfolio requirement.

Scholarships Offered

All applicants are automatically considered for merit scholarships. The Freshman Academic Achievement Scholarship awards $1,500-$10,000 based on high school academic performance. For more information, visit: https://www.limcollege.edu/admissions/financial-aid-options

Special Opportunities

LIM College offers various minors in Fashion Media, Fashion Merchandising, and Marketing. For more information, visit: https://www.limcollege.edu/academics/degrees/business-fashion-bba

Study abroad opportunities include affiliated programs in Italy and the Netherlands, exchange programs in England, France, Vietnam, and short term programs such as the Business + Culture trip in London and the Cross-Cultural Analysis Program in Europe.

Notable Alumni

- Leanne Gomez: Group Vice President at Ross Stores
- Daniella Vitale: Chief Executive Officer at Salvatore Ferragamo NA
- Florina Adili: Regional Vice President at Ulta Beauty

MARIST COLLEGE

Address: 3399 North Road, Poughkeepsie, NY 12601
Website: https://www.marist.edu/fashion-merchandising
Contact: https://www.marist.edu/admission/undergraduate/
counselors
Request for Information: https://www.marist.edu/request-
information
Phone: (845) 575-3000
Email: admission@marist.edu

COST OF ATTENDANCE:

Tuition & Fees: $44,360 | **Additional Expenses:** $20,075
Total: $64,435

Financial Aid: https://www.marist.edu/admission/student-
financial-services

ADDITIONAL INFORMATION:

Available Degree(s)

- BS in Fashion Merchandising, concentrations:
  - Business
  - Fashion Promotion
  - Product Development

Freshman Portfolio Requirement

There is no portfolio requirement.

Scholarships Offered

Merit-based scholarships at Marist College range from $10,000-
$25,000 per year. There is no additional application required. These
awards are renewable as long as students maintain a cumulative
GPA of 2.85. For more information, visit: https://www.marist.edu/
admission/financial-aid/marist-scholarships

Special Opportunities

There are semester and year-long study abroad programs at the
Marist campus in Florence, Italy and semesters in Paris and London
(with internship). In addition, a popular choice is the Marist in
Manhattan semester, which includes an intensive internship and
online study.

The Silver Needle Runway showcases student designers' works.
Approximately 2000 people attend. A presentation of awards
and scholarships follows the runway show. Awards have been
provided by Kate Spade, MPorium, Cutty Sark, and Young Menswear
Association, among others. For more information, visit: https://
www.marist.edu/communication-arts/fashion/silver-needle-runway

Notable Alumni

- Tara Bocchino: Product Management Director at Ralph
  Lauren
- Katelyn Salierno: Senior Manager of Design at Macy's

CONNECTICUT

MAINE

MASSACHUSETTS

NEW HAMPSHIRE

NEW JERSEY

NEW YORK

PENNSYLVANIA

RHODE ISLAND

VERMONT

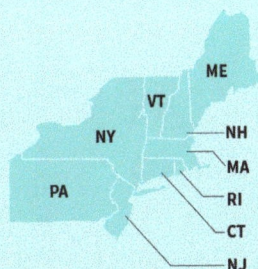

NORTHEAST

PARSONS - THE NEW SCHOOL

Address: 66 Fifth Avenue, New York, NY 10011
Website: https://www.newschool.edu/parsons/aas-fashion-marketing-communication/
Contact: https://www.newschool.edu/parsons/contact/
Request for Information: https://www.newschool.edu/parsons/contact-admissions/
Phone: (212) 229-8900
Email: thinkparsons@newschool.edu

COST OF ATTENDANCE:

Tuition & Fees: $51,722 | **Additional Expenses:** N/A
Total: $51,722

Financial Aid: https://www.newschool.edu/financial-aid/

ADDITIONAL INFORMATION:

Available Degree(s)

- AAS Fashion Marketing and Communication

Freshman Portfolio Requirement

- No portfolio requirement
- A one-page analysis of a fashion marketing campaign you find successful. (500-550 words)

For more information, visit: https://www.newschool.edu/parsons/how-to-apply-aas/

Scholarships Offered

The New School offers merit-based and need-based aid to students. Students are automatically considered for merit-based scholarships. These are based on the strength of the application and portfolio. Need-based aid is available to students who are eligible and submit the FAFSA. For more information, visit: https://www.newschool.edu/financial-aid/new-school-scholarships/

Notable Alumni

- Tom Ford: Designer and Filmmaker
- Reed Krakoff: Designer and Artistic Director at Tiffany
- Sara Little Turnbull: Design Consultant and Strategist

CONNECTICUT

MAINE

MASSACHUSETTS

NEW HAMPSHIRE

NEW JERSEY

NEW YORK

PENNSYLVANIA

RHODE ISLAND

VERMONT

DREXEL UNIVERSITY

Address: 3141 Chestnut Street, Philadelphia, PA 19104
Website: https://drexel.edu/westphal/academics/undergraduate/dsmr/
Contact: https://drexel.edu/westphal/about/contact/
Request for Information: https://drexel.edu/westphal/admissions/request-information/
Phone: (215) 895-2000
Email: westphal.admissions@drexel.edu

COST OF ATTENDANCE:

Tuition & Fees: $57,171 | **Additional Expenses:** $19,388
Total: $76,559

Financial Aid: https://drexel.edu/drexelcentral/finaid/overview/

ADDITIONAL INFORMATION:

Available Degree(s)

- BS in Design & Merchandising

Freshman Portfolio Requirement

- No portfolio requirement
- Writing supplement about why you are interested in pursuing the major (500 words max)

For more information, visit: https://drexel.edu/undergrad/apply/freshmen-instructions/

Scholarships Offered

Westphal Portfolio Scholarship is available to incoming first-year students based on outstanding portfolio work. Merit-based awards and other scholarships include a full-tuition scholarship for international studies offered by the Drexel Global Scholar program. For more information, visit: https://drexel.edu/drexelcentral/finaid/grants/undergraduate-scholarships/

Special Opportunities

Students may opt for a study abroad experience at London College of Fashion, the Accademia Italiana in Florence, or the Ecole Superiere de Commerce Exterieur (ESCE) in Paris.

Design & Merchandising majors may enroll in an accelerated dual degree program to earn a BS and a MBA in five years. For more information, visit: http://catalog.drexel.edu/undergraduate/collegeofmediaartsanddesign/design-and-merchandising_bsmba/index.html

Notable Alumni

- Bari Fisher: Senior Director of Global Operations at Anthropologie
- Jamie Peffley: Director of Global Sourcing at Party City
- Emily Engle: Digital Marketing Manager at Zilliant

CONNECTICUT

MAINE

MASSACHUSETTS

NEW HAMPSHIRE

NEW JERSEY

NEW YORK

PENNSYLVANIA

RHODE ISLAND

VERMONT

NORTHEAST

CONNECTICUT

MAINE

MASSACHUSETTS

NEW HAMPSHIRE

NEW JERSEY

NEW YORK

PENNSYLVANIA

RHODE ISLAND

VERMONT

THOMAS JEFFERSON UNIVERSITY

Address: 4201 Henry Avenue, Philadelphia, PA 19144
Website: https://www.jefferson.edu/academics/colleges-schools-institutes/kanbar-college-of-design-engineering-commerce/school-of-business/academic-programs/fashion-merchandising-management.html
Contact: https://www.jefferson.edu/university/contact.html
Request for Information: http://www.eastfalls.jefferson.edu/undergrad/Contact/requestinfo.html
Phone: (215) 951-2800
Email: Admissions@PhilaU.edu

COST OF ATTENDANCE:

Tuition & Fees: $42,966 | **Additional Expenses:** $14,949
Total: $57,925

Financial Aid: https://www.jefferson.edu/tuition-and-financial-aid.html

ADDITIONAL INFORMATION:

Available Degree(s)

- BS in Fashion Merchandising & Management

Freshman Portfolio Requirement

There is no portfolio requirement. However, freshman applicants of any major may submit an optional portfolio. For more information, visit: https://www.jefferson.edu/admissions/undergraduate/first-year/apply/portfolio-submission.html

Scholarships Offered

Thomas Jefferson University offers merit awards based on high school performance ranging from $8,000 to $23,000. There are also endowed scholarships for Fashion Merchandising & Management majors. For more information, visit: https://www.eastfalls.jefferson.edu/financialaid/Undergraduate/scholarships/index.html

Special Opportunities

An exclusive first-year program allows fashion merchandising and management students to participate in the Parisian fashion scene in the spring. Second year students have an opportunity to participate in the New York Immersion program.

Notable Alumni

- Jenee Sampson: Senior Buyer at QVC

UNIVERSITY OF RHODE ISLAND

Address: 35 Campus Avenue, Kingston, RI 02881
Website: https://web.uri.edu/business/about/tmd/
Contact: https://www.uri.edu/about/contact/
Request for Information: https://admissions.uri.edu/register/request-information
Phone: (401) 874-7000
Email: admission@uri.edu

COST OF ATTENDANCE:

In-State Tuition & Fees: $15,332 | **Additional Expenses:** $13,002
Total: $28,334

Out-of-State Tuition & Fees: $33,354 | **Additional Expenses:** $13,002
Total: $46,356

New England Regional Tuition: $25,270 | **Additional Expenses:** $13,002
Total: $38,272

Financial Aid: https://web.uri.edu/enrollment/financial-aid/

ADDITIONAL INFORMATION:

Available Degree(s)

- BS in Textiles, Fashion Merchandising, and Design, concentrations:
  - Fashion Merchandising
  - Apparel Design
  - Textile Science
- BS in Textile Marketing

Freshman Portfolio Requirement
There is no portfolio requirement.

Scholarships Offered
Applicants with a GPA of 3.2 or above will be considered for merit scholarships. The Thomas M. Ryan Scholars Program awards the full scholarships for all four years as well as resources such as the Honors Program and Colloquium. First-year applicants are also eligible for the URI Presidential Scholarship ($1,500- $15,000 per year) and the URI University Scholarship ($2,000-$10,000 per year). For more information, visit: https://web.uri.edu/admission/scholarships/

The BS in Textiles, Fashion Merchandising, and Design and the BS in Textile Marketing programs are part of the New England Regional Tuition Program, where students from New England states without a similar program get discounted tuition rates.

Special Opportunities
URI houses a library archive of 40,000+ commercial patterns and the Historic Textile and Costume Collection of 20,000+ items, one of the best collections in the country.

Popular study away opportunities include semester programs in London, Paris, and Florence, summer program at the Universite de la Mode in Lyon, France, and the New York experience.

Textiles, Fashion Merchandising and Design majors and Textile Marketing majors are eligible for the Accelerated B.S. to M.S. in Textiles, Fashion Merchandising, and Design program to earn both degrees in five years.

CONNECTICUT

MAINE

MASSACHUSETTS

NEW HAMPSHIRE

NEW JERSEY

NEW YORK

PENNSYLVANIA

RHODE ISLAND

VERMONT

NORTHEAST

ILLINOIS

INDIANA

IOWA

KANSAS

MICHIGAN

MINNESOTA

MISSOURI

NEBRASKA

NORTH DAKOTA

OHIO

SOUTH DAKOTA

WISCONSIN

CHAPTER 12

REGION TWO

MIDWEST

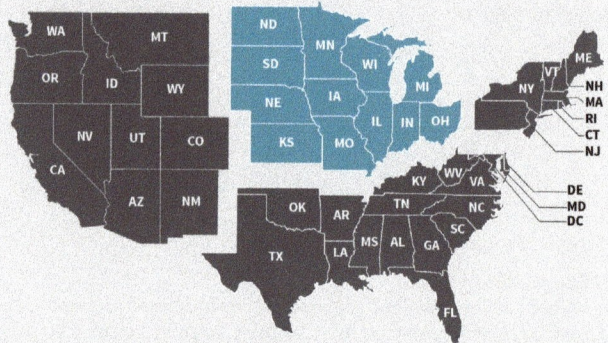

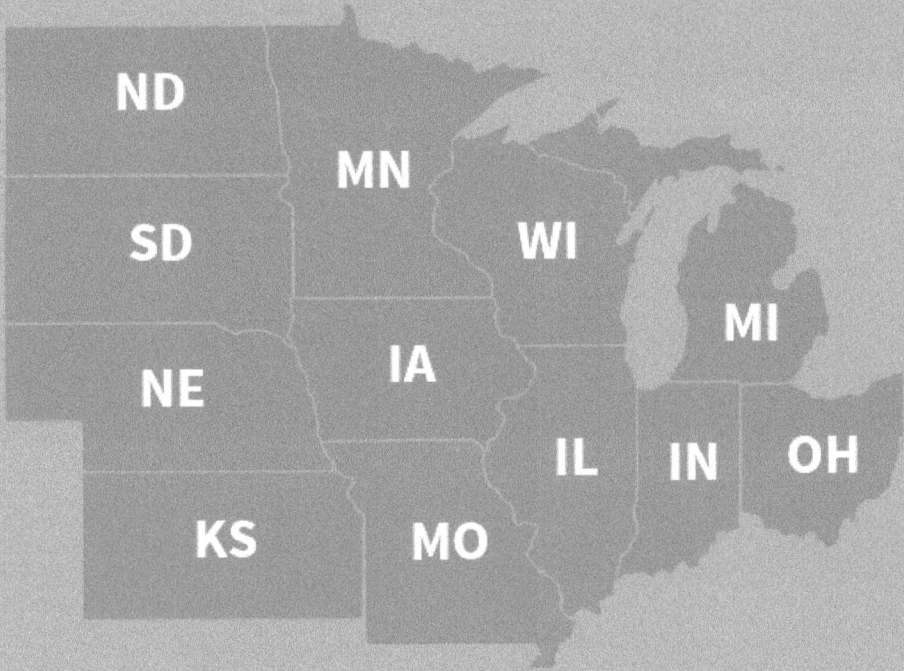

11 Programs | 12 States

1. IL - Columbia College Chicago
2. IL - Dominican University
3. IN - Indiana University at Bloomington
4. IA - Iowa State University
5. KS - Kansas State University
6. MN - University of Minnesota
7. MO - Stephens College
8. MO - University of Missouri
9. NE - University of Nebraska
10. OH - Kent State University
11. OH - Ohio State University

FASHION MERCHANDISING PROGRAMS

School	Avg. GPA, SAT Evidence-Based Reading Writing (ERW), SAT Math (M), and ACT Composite (C) Early Decision (ED): Yes/No	Admission Statistics	Program(s)	Portfolio and/ or Interview Required (Req.)
Columbia College Chicago 600 S. Michigan Avenue, Chicago, IL 60605	GPA: N/A SAT (ERW): N/A SAT (M): N/A ACT (C): N/A *Columbia College Chicago is test optional. ED: No	Admit Rate: 90% Undergrad Enrollment: 6,542 Total Enrollment: 6,769	BA in Fashion Studies, concentrations: Merchandising Product Development Degrees Awarded in the Program(s) (2020): 66	Portfolio: Not req. but strongly encouraged Interview: Not req.
Dominican University 7900 West Division Street, River Forest, IL 60305	GPA: 3.72 SAT (ERW): 480-580 SAT (M): 480-580 ACT (C): 19-24 ED: No	Admit Rate: 76% Undergrad Enrollment: 2,166 Total Enrollment: 3,189	BA in Fashion Merchandising Degrees Awarded in the Program(s) (2020): 14	Portfolio: Not req. Interview: Not req.
Indiana University at Bloomington 107 S. Indiana Avenue, Bloomington, IN 47405	GPA: 3.75 SAT (ERW): 560-670 SAT (M): 560-680 ACT (C): 24-31 *Indiana University at Bloomington is test optional. ED: No	Admit Rate: 80% Undergrad Enrollment: 32,986 Total Enrollment: 43,064	BS in Apparel Merchandising, concentrations: Digital Merchandising Product Development Degrees Awarded in the Program(s) (2020): 88	Portfolio: Not req. Interview: Not req.

School	Avg. GPA, SAT Evidence-Based Reading Writing (ERW), SAT Math (M), and ACT Composite (C) / Early Decision (ED): Yes/No	Admission Statistics	Program(s)	Portfolio and/ or Interview Required (Req.)
Iowa State University / 715 Bissell Rd., Ames, IA 50011	GPA: 3.71 / SAT (ERW): 480-630 / SAT (M): 530-680 / ACT (C): 21-28 / ED: No	Admit Rate: 88% / Undergrad Enrollment: 26,843 / Total Enrollment: 31,822	BS in Apparel, Merchandising, & Design, options in: / Product Management and Sourcing / Merchandising and Retail Analytics / Fashion Communication / Degrees Awarded in the Program(s) (2020): N/A	Portfolio: Not req. / Interview: Not req.
Kansas State University / 225 Justin Hall, 1324 Lovers Lane, Manhattan, KS 66506	GPA: 3.62 / SAT (ERW): N/A / SAT (M): N/A / ACT (C): 20-27 / *Kansas State University is test optional. / ED: No	Admit Rate: 94% / Undergrad Enrollment: 16,257 / Total Enrollment: 20,854	BS in Fashion Studies, specialization: Fashion Business / Degrees Awarded in the Program(s) (2020): 58	Portfolio: Not req. / Interview: Not req.

MIDWEST

FASHION MERCHANDISING PROGRAMS

School	Avg. GPA, SAT Evidence-Based Reading Writing (ERW), SAT Math (M), and ACT Composite (C) Early Decision (ED): Yes/No	Admission Statistics	Program(s)	Portfolio and/or Interview Required (Req.)
University of Minnesota 107 Rapson Hall, 89 Church Street SE, Minneapolis, MN 55455	GPA: N/A SAT (ERW): 600-700 SAT (M): 640-760 ACT (C): 25-31 ED: No	Admit Rate: 70% Undergrad Enrollment: 36,061 Total Enrollment: 52,017	BS in Retail Merchandising Degrees Awarded in the Program(s) (2020): 15	Portfolio: Not req. Interview: Not req.
Stephens College 1200 E Broadway, Columbia, MO 65215	GPA: N/A SAT (ERW): 600-700 SAT (M): 640-760 ACT (C): 25-31 ED: No	Admit Rate: 64% Undergrad Enrollment: 443 Total Enrollment: 622	BS in Fashion Marketing and Management BFA in Fashion Communication Degrees Awarded in the Program(s) (2020): 13	Portfolio: Not req. Interview: Not req.
University of Missouri 317 Lowry Hall. University of Missouri. Columbia, MO 65211	GPA: N/A SAT (ERW): 560-660 SAT (M): 550-660 ACT (C): 23-29 ED: No	Admit Rate: 82% Undergrad Enrollment: 23,383 Total Enrollment: 31,089	BS in Textile and Apparel Management, tracks: Apparel Retailing and Digital Merchandising Apparel Product Development Degrees Awarded in the Program(s) (2020): N/A	Portfolio: Not req. Interview: Not req.

School	Avg. GPA, SAT Evidence-Based Reading Writing (ERW), SAT Math (M), and ACT Composite (C) Early Decision (ED): Yes/No	Admission Statistics	Program(s)	Portfolio and/ or Interview Required (Req.)
University of Nebraska 4th and R St, Lincoln, NE 68588	GPA: 3.6 SAT (ERW): 550-650 SAT (M): 560-670 ACT (C): 22-28 ED: No	Admit Rate: 78% Undergrad Enrollment: 20,286 Total Enrollment: 25,108	BS in Merchandising BS in Textiles, Merchandising & Fashion Design/ Communications Degrees Awarded in the Program(s) (2020): 15	Portfolio: Not req. Interview: Not req.
Kent State University 515 Hilltop Drive, Kent, OH 44242	GPA: 3.61 SAT (ERW): 510-610 SAT (M): 510-600 ACT (C): 20-26 ED: No	Admit Rate: 84% Undergrad Enrollment: 21,621 Total Enrollment: 26,822	BS in Fashion Merchandising BS/MBA in Fashion Merchandising Degrees Awarded in the Program(s) (2020): 100 (Fashion Design); 309 (Fashion Merchandising)	Portfolio: Not req. Interview: Not req.
The Ohio State University 172 Arps Hall, 1945 N. High Street, Columbus, OH 43210	GPA: N/A SAT (ERW): 590-690 SAT (M): 620-740 ACT (C): 26-32 ED: No	Admit Rate: 68% Undergrad Enrollment: 46,984 Total Enrollment: 61,369	BS in Fashion and Retail Studies Degrees Awarded in the Program(s) (2020): 77	Portfolio: Not req. Interview: Not req.

MIDWEST

ILLINOIS

INDIANA

IOWA

KANSAS

MICHIGAN

MINNESOTA

MISSOURI

NEBRASKA

NORTH DAKOTA

OHIO

SOUTH DAKOTA

WISCONSIN

COLUMBIA COLLEGE CHICAGO

Address: 600 S. Michigan Avenue, Chicago, IL 60605
Website: https://www.colum.edu/academics/programs/fashion-studies
Contact: https://www.colum.edu/contact
Request for Information: https://apply.colum.edu/register/moreinfo
Phone: (312) 369-1000
Email: admissions@colum.edu

COST OF ATTENDANCE:

Tuition & Fees: $35,716 | **Additional Expenses:** $18,000
Total: $53,716

Financial Aid: https://www.colum.edu/columbia-central/where-to-start/index

ADDITIONAL INFORMATION:

Available Degree(s)

- BA in Fashion Studies, concentrations:
  o Merchandising
  o Product Development

Freshman Portfolio Requirement

Portfolios are optional for all applications that apply to a BA program at Columbia College Chicago. Applicants are encouraged to submit a portfolio not only for admission to their desired program but also for the Faculty Recognition Award.

- Submit 10 annotated images in PDF format that demonstrate how you engage with fashion as a practice or industry
- May include drawings, product curation, color study work, materials investigation, styling, garments, digital media, etc.

For more information, visit: https://www.colum.edu/admissions/additional-information/portfolio-and-audition-requirements

Scholarships Offered

Applicants including international students are automatically considered for talent-based scholarships. A digital portfolio or audition is required. Many internal scholarships are awarded to local high school graduates. For more information, visit: https://www.colum.edu/columbia-central/scholarships/index

Special Opportunities

Faculty-led study away opportunities for Fashion Studies students include Marketing in Europe: Paris, Bath Spa Textile Techniques Immersion, Fashion Studies in the Field: New York, Global Marketing: Prague and Berlin Street Style. Students can also spend a semester as an exchange student at Flinders University in Adelaide, South Australia and University of East London.

Notable Alumni

- Roma Shah: Wholesale Manager at Saint Laurent
- Alexander Knox: Fashion Designer at Coach
- Paul Anthony Lopacinski: Senior Manager Special Productions at Macy's

DOMINICAN UNIVERSITY

Address: 7900 West Division Street, River Forest, IL 60305
Website: https://www.dom.edu/academics/majors-programs/
fashion-merchandising
Contact: https://www.dom.edu/about-dominican/contact-us
Request for Information: https://www.dom.edu/admission/
request-information
Phone: (708) 366-2490
Email: domadmis@dom.edu

COST OF ATTENDANCE:

Tuition & Fees: $36,500 | **Additional Expenses:** $13,622
Total: $50,122

Financial Aid: https://www.dom.edu/admission/office-financial-aid

ADDITIONAL INFORMATION:

Available Degree(s)

- BA in Fashion Merchandising

Freshman Portfolio Requirement

There is no portfolio requirement.

Scholarships Offered

Dominican University offers various scholarships, including the
Freshman Merit Scholarships based on academic performance,
which ranges from $10,000 to $20,000 annually. For more
information, visit: https://www.dom.edu/admission/scholarships-
dominican#undergraduate

Special Opportunities

Paris: Essentials of French Fashion is an exclusive study away
program for Fashion students which provides an immersed
experience from a French fashion perspective at the Paris American
Academy. Students can also spend a semester or a year at Milan's
Instituto di Moda Burgo or take a trip to New York City sponsored by
the Fashion department.

Notable Alumni

- Danielle Moorhouse: Visual Merchandising Manager at
  Anthropologie
- Sabrina Gaeta: Retail Sales Manager at Nordstrom
- Carin Carey: District Manager at Nordstrom

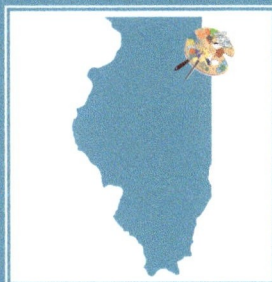

ILLINOIS

INDIANA

IOWA

KANSAS

MICHIGAN

MINNESOTA

MISSOURI

NEBRASKA

NORTH DAKOTA

OHIO

SOUTH DAKOTA

WISCONSIN

MIDWEST

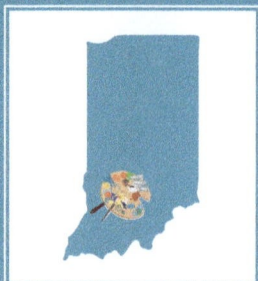

INDIANA UNIVERSITY AT BLOOMINGTON

Address: 107 S. Indiana Avenue, Bloomington, IN 47405
Website: https://college.indiana.edu/academics/degrees-majors/major-guides/apparel-merchandising-bs.html
Contact: https://admissions.indiana.edu/contact/index.html
Request for Information: N/A
Phone: (812) 855-4848
Email: admissions@indiana.edu

COST OF ATTENDANCE:

In-State Tuition & Fees: $11,332 | **Additional Expenses:** $15,966
Total: $27,298

Out-of-State Tuition & Fees: $38,352 | **Additional Expenses:** $15,966
Total: $54,318

Financial Aid: https://admissions.indiana.edu/cost-financial-aid/financial-aid.html

ADDITIONAL INFORMATION:

Available Degree(s)

- BS in Apparel Merchandising, concentrations:
  o Digital Merchandising
  o Product Development

Freshman Portfolio Requirement

There is no portfolio requirement.

Scholarships Offered

Indiana University Bloomington offers a variety of scholarships for in-state, out-of-state, and international students. Students applying before the early action deadline will receive consideration for IU Academic Scholarships ($1,000–$11,000) and for the invitation-only Selective Scholarship. For more information, visit: https://scholarships.indiana.edu/future-scholars/first-year-scholarships.html

U.S. citizens with Apparel Merchandising as their intended major are eligible for the Lois Eskenazi Scholarship, which awards $3,000 a year.

Special Opportunities

High-achieving students may be eligible for Academic Excellence within the College of Arts and Sciences or for admission to the Hutton Honors College.

Study abroad opportunities include the faculty-led Sustainable Products summer program in Guatemala and the Fashion & Art: Italian Artisanal Design & Branding summer program in Rome, Florence, and Milan.

Notable Alumni

- Alexa Silverman: Director of Site Merchandising, Fragrances at Macy's
- Briana Byrd: Merchandise Manager at Kohl's Department Stores
- Morton Jennifer: Sr. Buyer at Kohl's Department Stores

ILLINOIS

INDIANA

IOWA

KANSAS

MICHIGAN

MINNESOTA

MISSOURI

NEBRASKA

NORTH DAKOTA

OHIO

SOUTH DAKOTA

WISCONSIN

IOWA STATE UNIVERSITY

Address: 715 Bissell Rd, Ames, IA 50011
Website: https://www.hs.iastate.edu/find-majors/fashion_textiles/
Contact: https://www.admissions.iastate.edu/contact_us.php
Request for Information: https://www.admissions.iastate.edu/request_info.php
Phone: (515) 294-4111
Email: admissions@iastate.edu

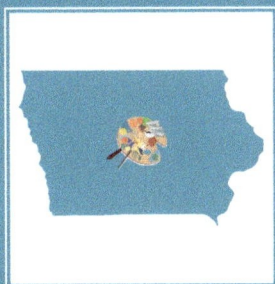

COST OF ATTENDANCE:

In-State Tuition & Fees: $9,634 | **Additional Expenses:** $12,518
Total: $22,152

Out-of-State Tuition & Fees: $25,446 | **Additional Expenses:** $12,518
Total: $37,964

Financial Aid: https://www.financialaid.iastate.edu/

ADDITIONAL INFORMATION:

Available Degree(s)

- BS in Apparel, Merchandising, & Design, options in:
  - Product Management and Sourcing
  - Merchandising and Retail Analytics
  - Fashion Communication

Freshman Portfolio Requirement

There is no portfolio requirement.

Scholarships Offered

Iowa State offers merit-based scholarships based on GPA and ACT/SAT. Award amounts/criteria may vary from state to state. To review available awards by your state, visit: https://www.admissions.iastate.edu/scholarships/freshman.php

Automatic scholarships for international students that meet specific GPA and SAT/ACT combination include the President's Award for International Student Excellence $12,000 a year.

Special Opportunities

ISU houses numerous high-tech equipment, such as a 3D body scanner, an industrial digital printer, and state-of-the-art design software. Facilities include a textiles conservation laboratory, a historical garment collection, an apparel production center, and a clothing museum.

Apparel, Merchandising, & Design majors may study abroad at London College of Fashion, Glasgow Caledonian University, Paris American Academy, Lorenzo de' Medici Institute, and Accademia Italiana.

Notable Alumni

- Todd Snyder: Founder of Todd Snyder clothing company and Co-Founder of Tailgate Clothing Company

ILLINOIS

INDIANA

IOWA

KANSAS

MICHIGAN

MINNESOTA

MISSOURI

NEBRASKA

NORTH DAKOTA

OHIO

SOUTH DAKOTA

WISCONSIN

MIDWEST

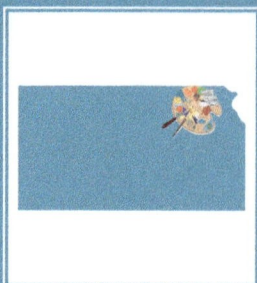

ILLINOIS

INDIANA

IOWA

KANSAS

MICHIGAN

MINNESOTA

MISSOURI

NEBRASKA

NORTH DAKOTA

OHIO

SOUTH DAKOTA

WISCONSIN

KANSAS STATE UNIVERSITY

Address: 225 Justin Hall, 1324 Lovers Lane, Manhattan, KS 66506
Website: https://www.k-state.edu/academics/majors-programs/fashion-studies-degree/
Contact: https://www.k-state.edu/contact/
Request for Information: https://www.k-state.edu/admission/request-info/
Phone: (785) 532-6993
Email: idfsinfo@k-state.edu

COST OF ATTENDANCE:

In-State Tuition & Fees: $12,560 | **Additional Expenses:** $15,310
Total: $27,870

Out-of-State Tuition & Fees: $28,754 | **Additional Expenses:** $15,636
Total: $44,390

Financial Aid: https://www.k-state.edu/sfa/

ADDITIONAL INFORMATION:

Available Degree(s)
- BS in Fashion Studies, specialization: Fashion Business

Freshman Portfolio Requirement
There is no portfolio requirement.

Scholarships Offered
Kansas State University offers general scholarships with criteria varying from state to state. Students from certain states are eligible for the Midwest Student Exchange Program (a $45,306 tuition reduction over 4 years). K-State also offers test-optional and competitive awards. To review available awards by your state, visit: https://www.k-state.edu/sfa/scholarships-aid/scholarships/future-students/

International students may receive awards ranging from $8,000-$32,000 over four years. For more information, visit: https://www.k-state.edu/sfa/aid/scholarships/future-students/

FASH Scholarships include awards gained via competitions through professional organizations. These competitions include the National Retail Federation Scholarships. For more information, visit: https://www.hhs.k-state.edu/idfs/current-students/fashion-studies-scholarships/

Special Opportunities
All apparel and textiles students are required to participate in a 260-hour internship completed over Junior or Senior year. Internship locations in the past have included Gucci, J. Crew, Nordstrom, and Kohl's, among others. Students have worked in internships nationwide and internationally (UK, China, South Korea, India, and Nepal).

Students are encouraged to participate in study abroad on one of the regularly scheduled faculty-led study tours in England, Italy, and Denmark. For more information, visit: https://www.k-state.edu/abroad/documents/maps/interiordesignfashionstudies.pdf

Notable Alumni
- Andrea Albright: Merchandising Senior Vice President at Walmart
- Jami Dunbar: Senior Vice President of Global Product Supply at Under Armour
- Avery Sims: Director of Merchandising at Design Resources, Inc.

UNIVERSITY OF MINNESOTA

Address: 240 McNeal Hall, 1985 Buford Ave., St Paul, MN 55108
Website: https://design.umn.edu/academics/programs/retail-merchandising/retail-merchandising-bs
Contact: http://umn.force.com/admissions/
Request for Information: N/A
Phone: (612) 624-9700
Email: cdesinfo@umn.edu

COST OF ATTENDANCE:

In-State Tuition & Fees: $15,368 | **Additional Expenses:** $14,316
Total: $29,684

Out-of-State Tuition & Fees: $33,958 | **Additional Expenses:** $15,816
Total: $49,774

Financial Aid: https://admissions.tc.umn.edu/costsaid/index.html

ADDITIONAL INFORMATION:

Available Degree(s)

- BS in Retail Merchandising

Freshman Portfolio Requirement

There is no portfolio requirement.

Scholarships Offered

University of Minnesota offers numerous scholarship opportunities to all students, including in-state and out-of-state students. All international students are automatically considered for the Global Excellence Scholarship ($10,000-$25,000 per year for up to four years). For more information, visit: https://admissions.tc.umn.edu/costsaid/scholarships.html

Retail Merchandising students are eligible for the Sylvia and Sam Druy Scholarship ($1,000-$3,000) and the Legacy Scholarship ($1,500-$3,000 per year for four years). For more information, visit: https://admissions.tc.umn.edu/cost-aid/scholarships/college-specific-scholarships#cdes

Special Opportunities

Through learning abroad programs, students may travel to Shanghai, China, study Business & International Affairs in Paris, intern in London and Florence. Students may also participate in the annual National Retail Federation Student Program in New York City.

Notable Alumni

- Robert Ulrich: Former CEO at Target
- Michael P. Sullivan: Former President at Dairy Queen
- Jill Konrath: Sales Strategist and Author of Selling to Big Companies and SNAP Selling

ILLINOIS

INDIANA

IOWA

KANSAS

MICHIGAN

MINNESOTA

MISSOURI

NEBRASKA

NORTH DAKOTA

OHIO

SOUTH DAKOTA

WISCONSIN

MIDWEST

ILLINOIS

INDIANA

IOWA

KANSAS

MICHIGAN

MINNESOTA

MISSOURI

NEBRASKA

NORTH DAKOTA

OHIO

SOUTH DAKOTA

WISCONSIN

STEPHENS COLLEGE

Address: 1200 E Broadway, Columbia, MO 65215
Website: https://www.stephens.edu/academics/undergraduate-programs/fashion-marketing-management/
Contact: https://www.stephens.edu/campus-offices/
Request for Information: https://stephenscollege.secure.force.com/form?formid=217721
Phone: (573) 442-2211
Email: info@stephens.edu

COST OF ATTENDANCE:

Tuition & Fees: $23,385 | **Additional Expenses:** $12,864
Total: $36,249

Financial Aid: https://www.stephens.edu/admission-aid/undergraduate/financial-aid/

ADDITIONAL INFORMATION:

Available Degree(s)

- BS in Fashion Marketing and Management
- BFA in Fashion Communication

Freshman Portfolio Requirement

There is no portfolio requirement.

Scholarships Offered

Stephens College offers various institutional merit-based scholarships for incoming freshmen. The Academic Merit Scholarship awards $7,000 up to full tuition and is renewable for four years. For more information, visit: https://www.stephens.edu/admission-aid/undergraduate/financial-aid/first-year-scholarships/

Special Opportunities

The Stephens College Costume Museum and Research Library archives more than 13,000 historical garments and accessories, with pieces dating back to 1730.

Fashion students may study abroad through the DIS Study Abroad in Scandinavia program and the Study Abroad Italy program or directly enroll in the Accademia Italiana.

Notable Alumni

- Bonnie McElveen-Hunter: Founder and CEO of Pace Communications and Former U.S. Ambassador to Finland

UNIVERSITY OF MISSOURI

Address: University of Missouri, Columbia, MO 65211
Website: https://majors.missouri.edu/textile-and-apparel-management-bs/
Contact: https://admissions.missouri.edu/contact/
Request for Information: https://admissions.missouri.edu/contact/
Phone: (573) 882-7786
Email: askmizzou@missouri.edu

COST OF ATTENDANCE:

In-State Tuition & Fees: $13,128 | **Additional Expenses:** $10,964
Total: $24,092

Out-of-State Tuition & Fees: $31,734 | **Additional Expenses:** $10,964
Total: $42,698

Financial Aid: https://admissions.missouri.edu/financial-aid/

ADDITIONAL INFORMATION:

Available Degree(s)

- BS in Textile and Apparel Management, tracks:
  o Apparel Retailing and Digital Merchandising
  o Apparel Product Development

Freshman Portfolio Requirement

There is no portfolio requirement.

Scholarships Offered

University of Missouri offers automatic scholarships to in-state students, out-of-state students, and international students. Applicants who apply test-optional and do not have official test scores are reviewed holistically for scholarships. Competitive awards include the Stamps Scholars Award (full scholarship). For more information, visit: https://admissions.missouri.edu/scholarships/

The Department of Textile & Apparel Management awards numerous scholarships to Textile and Apparel Management majors. For more information, visit: https://tam.missouri.edu/undergraduate/department-scholarships/

Special Opportunities

University of Missouri houses the Missouri Historic Costume and Textile Collection, which is home to more than 7,000 dress and textile artifacts ranging in date from the nineteenth to the twenty-first centuries as well as 4,000 archival resources including books, magazines, illustrations, and photographs.

Study away opportunities for Textile and Apparel Management students include immersion programs in El Salvador, China, England, France, and Italy as well as a New York City study tour.

Notable Alumni

- Sam Walton: Founder of Walmart
- Robin Luke: Professor and Head of Marketing Department at Missouri State University

ILLINOIS

INDIANA

IOWA

KANSAS

MICHIGAN

MINNESOTA

MISSOURI

NEBRASKA

NORTH DAKOTA

OHIO

SOUTH DAKOTA

WISCONSIN

MIDWEST

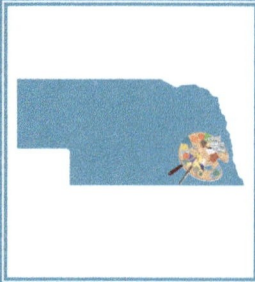

ILLINOIS

INDIANA

IOWA

KANSAS

MICHIGAN

MINNESOTA

MISSOURI

NEBRASKA

NORTH DAKOTA

OHIO

SOUTH DAKOTA

WISCONSIN

UNIVERSITY OF NEBRASKA

Address: 4th and R St, Lincoln, NE 68588
Website: https://cehs.unl.edu/tmfd/
Contact: https://admissions.unl.edu/contact-us/
Request for Information: N/A
Phone: (402) 472-2023
Email: admissions@unl.edu

COST OF ATTENDANCE:

In-State Tuition & Fees: $7,770 | **Additional Expenses:** $14,242
Total: $22,012

Out-of-State Tuition & Fees: $24,900 | **Additional Expenses:** $14,242
Total: $39,142

Financial Aid: https://admissions.unl.edu/cost/#financial-aid

ADDITIONAL INFORMATION:

Available Degree(s)

- BS in Merchandising
- BS in Textiles, Merchandising & Fashion Design/ Communications

Freshman Portfolio Requirement

There is no portfolio requirement.

Scholarships Offered

Most first-year scholarships are based on high school GPA. Leadership, service, and diversity scholarships are based on holistic review. The Chancellor's Tuition Scholarship awards full tuition and is open to both in-state students and out-of-state students. For more information, visit: https://admissions.unl.edu/cost/

Special Opportunities

The Department of Textiles, Merchandising, and Fashion Design's Historic Textile and Costume Collections archive over 3,500 textiles, garments, and accessories that represent 19th and 20th century dress, with emphasis on 20th century American designers.

Department-sponsored study away opportunities include the Annual Summer Sessions study tours that alternate in a three-year cycle in New York City, Europe (Paris, London, Prague, Milan), and Asia (Shanghai and Beijing). Students may also spend a semester abroad at Lorenzo de' Medici, the Italian International Institute, American Intercontinental University, and University of the Arts, London.

Notable Alumni

- Kiersten Runnels: Merchandising Field Leader at Apple
- Eulanda Sanders: Professor and Chair of the Department of Apparel, Events, and Hospitality Management at Iowa State University
- LynDee Lombardo: Executive Committee Chair for Membership and Marketing at Washington Association of Family and Consumer Sciences

KENT STATE UNIVERSITY

Address: 515 Hilltop Drive, Kent, OH 44242
Website: https://www.kent.edu/fashion
Contact: https://www.kent.edu/theatredance/contact-us
Request for Information: https://ksu.secure.force.com/
form/?formid=217802
Phone: (330) 672-2082
Email: theatre@kent.edu

COST OF ATTENDANCE:

In-State Tuition & Fees: $11,923 | **Additional Expenses:** $17,745
Total: $29,668

Out-of-State Tuition & Fees: $20,799 | **Additional Expenses:** $17,745
Total: $38,544

Financial Aid: https://www.kent.edu/financialaid

ADDITIONAL INFORMATION:

Available Degree(s)
- BS in Fashion Merchandising
- BS/MBA in Fashion Merchandising

Freshman Portfolio Requirement
There is no portfolio requirement. Students applying to the Fashion
Merchandising program must have at least a 3.0 cumulative
GPA and a minimum ACT composite score of 21+ or SAT total
score of 1060+. Students who cannot meet these criteria will not
be accepted into the programs but may be eligible to the pre-
fashion design and merchandising non-degree major (PFDM).
These students may declare a fashion merchandising major
after completing 12+ hours of college-level coursework at Kent
State with a cumulative GPA of 2.75+.For more information, visit:
https://www.kent.edu/admissions/undergraduate/fashion-design-
merchandising

Scholarships Offered
Both in-state and out-of-state applicants are eligible for merit-
based awards, including the President's Achievement Award ($1,000
- $4,000 for in-state students and $4,000-$12,500 for out-of-state
students), the Honors Distinction Award ($2,000), and the Founders
Scholarship ($1,000-$2,000). For more information, visit: https://
www.kent.edu/scholarships

60 scholarship opportunities are offered to School of Fashion
students. For more information, visit: https://www.kent.edu/
fashion/scholarships

Special Opportunities
The Kent State University Museum holds collections of historic
dress, fashion, textiles, and decorative arts, where students can find
works by many of the world's great artists and designers.

The Summer Fashion Academy allows high school students to
explore key areas in fashion merchandising.

Kent State School of Fashion offers semester programs as well
as a summer program at its NYC campus. Other study away
opportunities have brought students to Los Angeles, Prais,
Florence, and Hong Kong.

The School of Fashion offers a minor in Fashion Media.

Notable Alumni
- Stephen "Suede" Baum: Fashion
  Designer and Contestant on Project
  Runway and Project Runway: All Stars

ILLINOIS

INDIANA

IOWA

KANSAS

MICHIGAN

MINNESOTA

MISSOURI

NEBRASKA

NORTH DAKOTA

OHIO

SOUTH DAKOTA

WISCONSIN

MIDWEST

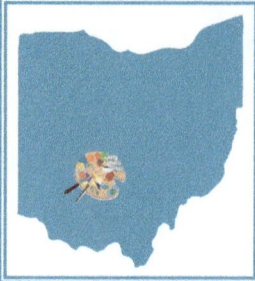

ILLINOIS

INDIANA

IOWA

KANSAS

MICHIGAN

MINNESOTA

MISSOURI

NEBRASKA

NORTH DAKOTA

OHIO

SOUTH DAKOTA

WISCONSIN

THE OHIO STATE UNIVERSITY

Address: 1849 Cannon Drive, Columbus, OH 43210
Website: https://ehe.osu.edu/human-sciences/consumer-sciences/fashion-and-retail/bs/
Contact: https://theatre.osu.edu/contact
Request for Information: N/A
Phone: (614) 292-5821
Email: theatre-ugrad@osu.edu

COST OF ATTENDANCE:

In-State Tuition & Fees: $11,936 | **Additional Expenses:** $17,086
Total: $29,022

Out-of-State Tuition & Fees: $35,018 | **Additional Expenses:** $17,904
Total: $52,922

Financial Aid: https://sfa.osu.edu/

ADDITIONAL INFORMATION:

Available Degree(s)

- BS in Fashion and Retail Studies

Freshman Portfolio Requirement

There is no portfolio requirement.

Scholarships Offered

University merit scholarships include the Eminence Fellows Program and Scholarship (full cost of attendance for 8 semesters plus an enrichment grant valued at up to $3,000), the Morrill Scholarship Program, the Maximus Scholarship. For more information, visit: http://undergrad.osu.edu/cost-and-aid/merit-based-scholarships

Special Opportunities

The Historic Costume & Textiles Collection holds more than 11,500 objects from the mid-18th century to contemporary 21st century designers as well as numerous period fashion magazines, fashion plates, swatch books and commercial patterns.

Notable Alumni

- Martin Keen: Design Director and Founder at Focal Upright Furniture
- Peter Michailidis: Founder at The Streamable and Director at Nōwn
- Walden O'Dell: CEO of Diebold

ALABAMA

ARKANSAS

DELAWARE

DISTRICT OF
COLUMBIA

FLORIDA

GEORGIA

KENTUCKY

LOUISIANA

MARYLAND

MISSISSIPPI

NORTH CAROLINA

OKLAHOMA

SOUTH CAROLINA

TENNESSEE

TEXAS

VIRGINIA

WEST VIRGINIA

CHAPTER 13

REGION THREE

SOUTH

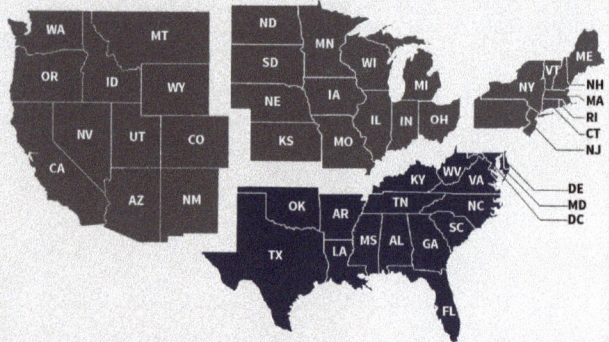

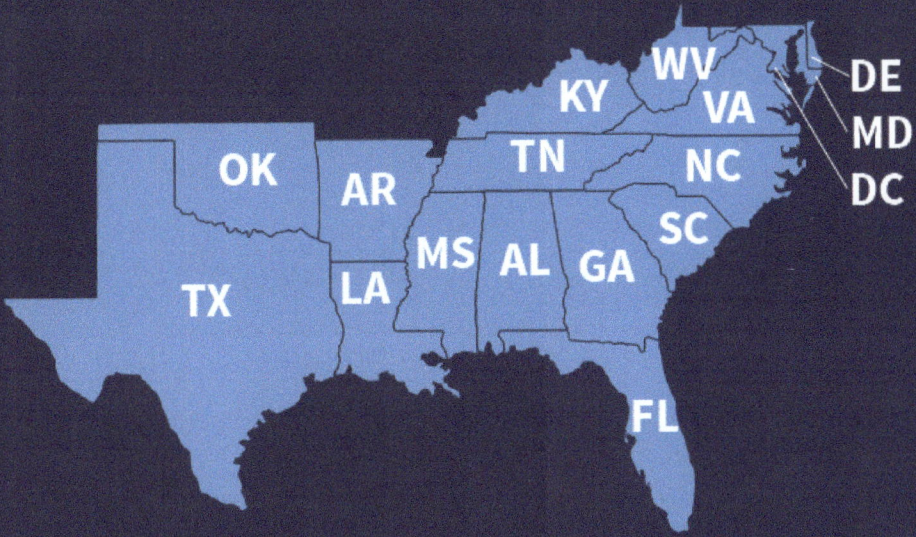

21 Programs | 16 States

1. AL - Auburn University
2. DE - University of Delaware
3. FL - Florida State University
4. FL - Miami International University Art & Design
5. GA - Savannah College of Art & Design (SCAD)
6. GA - University of Georgia
7. LA - Louisiana State University
8. NC - North Carolina State University, Raleigh College of Design
9. NC - University of North Carolina, Greensboro
10. OK - Oklahoma State University
11. SC - University of South Carolina
12. TX - Baylor University
13. TX - Southern Methodist University (SMU)
14. TX - Texas Tech University
15. TX - Texas Woman's University
16. TX - University of North Texas
17. TX - University of Texas, Austin (UT Austin)
18. TX - University of the Incarnate Word
19. VA - Virginia Commonwealth University
20. VA - Virginia Tech University
21. WV - West Virginia University

School	Avg. GPA, SAT Evidence-Based Reading Writing (ERW), SAT Math (M), and ACT Composite (C) Early Decision (ED): Yes/No	Admission Statistics	Program(s)	Portfolio and/ or Interview Required (Req.)
Auburn University 210 Spidle Hall, Auburn, AL 36849	GPA: 3.97 SAT (ERW): 590-650 SAT (M): 570-670 ACT (C): 25-31 ED: No	Admit Rate: 85% Undergrad Enrollment: 24,505 Total Enrollment: 30,737	BS in Apparel Merchandising, Design, and Production Management, options in: Merchandising Apparel Design and Production Management Degrees Awarded in the Program(s) (2020): N/A	Portfolio: Not req. Interview: Not req.
University of Delaware 211 Alison Hall West, University of Delaware, Newark, DE 19716	GPA: 3.92 SAT (ERW): 580-660 SAT (M): 570-670 ACT (C): 25-30 ED: No	Admit Rate: 66% Undergrad Enrollment: 19,328 Total Enrollment: 23,613	BS in Fashion Merchandising and Management Degrees Awarded in the Program(s) (2020): 10	Portfolio: Not req. Interview: Not req.
Florida State University Roderick K. Shaw Building (RSB), 644 West Call Street, Tallahassee, FL 32306-1115	GPA: 4.16 SAT (ERW): 620-680 SAT (M): 600-670 ACT (C): 27-31 ED: No	Admit Rate: 32% Undergrad Enrollment: 32,543 Total Enrollment: 43,569	BS in Retail Entrepreneurship, tracks: Retail Merchandising Product Development Degrees Awarded in the Program(s) (2020): 93	Portfolio: Not req. Interview: Not req.

School	Avg. GPA, SAT Evidence-Based Reading Writing (ERW), SAT Math (M), and ACT Composite (C) Early Decision (ED): Yes/No	Admission Statistics	Program(s)	Portfolio and/or Interview Required (Req.)
Miami International University Art & Design 1501 Biscayne Blvd Suite 100, Miami, FL 33132	GPA: N/A SAT (ERW): N/A SAT (M): N/A ACT (C): N/A *Miami International University Art & Design has an open admissions policy. ED: No	Admit Rate: N/A Undergrad Enrollment: 874 Total Enrollment: 934	BA in Fashion Merchandising Degrees Awarded in the Program(s) (2020): 5	Portfolio: Not req. Interview: Not req.
Savannah College of Art & Design (SCAD) 342 Bull St., Savannah, GA 31401	GPA: 3.6 SAT (ERW): 540-640 SAT (M): 500-600 ACT (C): 20-27 ED: No	Admit Rate: 78% Undergrad Enrollment: 11,679 Total Enrollment: 14,265	BFA in Fashion Marketing and Management Degrees Awarded in the Program(s) (2020): 120	Portfolio: Optional, required for scholarship consideration Interview: Not req.
University of Georgia Dawson Hall, 305 Sanford Dr., Athens, GA 30602	GPA: 4.02 SAT (ERW): 620-700 SAT (M): 600-720 ACT (C): ED: No	Admit Rate: 48% Undergrad Enrollment: 29,765 Total Enrollment: 39,147	BS in Fashion Merchandising, emphasis: Fashion Brand Management Degrees Awarded in the Program(s) (2020): 63	Portfolio: Not req. Interview: Not req.

School	Avg. GPA, SAT Evidence-Based Reading Writing (ERW), SAT Math (M), and ACT Composite (C) Early Decision (ED): Yes/No	Admission Statistics	Program(s)	Portfolio and/ or Interview Required (Req.)
Louisiana State University Louisiana State University, Baton Rouge, LA 70803	GPA: 3.45 SAT (ERW): 550-660 SAT (M): 540-640 ACT (C): 23-28 ED: No	Admit Rate: 73% Undergrad Enrollment: 27,825 Total Enrollment: 34,285	BS in Textiles, Apparel, & Merchandising, concentration: Merchandising Degrees Awarded in the Program(s) (2020): 40	Portfolio: Not req. Interview: Not req.
North Carolina State University, Raleigh College of Design 1020 Main Campus Dr., Raleigh, NC 27606	GPA: 3.8 SAT (ERW): 620-690 SAT (M): 630-730 ACT (C): 27-32 ED: No	Admit Rate: 46% Undergrad Enrollment: 26,150 Total Enrollment: 36,042	BS in Fashion and Textile Management, concentrations: Fashion Development and Product Management Brand Management and Marketing Degrees Awarded in the Program(s) (2020): N/A	Portfolio: Not req. Interview: Not req.
University of North Carolina, Greensboro 210 Stone Building, PO Box 26170, Greensboro, NC 27402-6170	GPA: 3.67 SAT (ERW): 490-590 SAT (M): 490-570 ACT (C): 19-25 ED: No	Admit Rate: 88% Undergrad Enrollment: 15,995 Total Enrollment: 19,764	BS in Consumer, Apparel, and Retail Studies, concentration: Retailing and Consumer Studies Degrees Awarded in the Program(s) (2020): 76	Portfolio: Not req. Interview: Not req.

School	Avg. GPA, SAT Evidence-Based Reading Writing (ERW), SAT Math (M), and ACT Composite (C) Early Decision (ED): Yes/No	Admission Statistics	Program(s)	Portfolio and/or Interview Required (Req.)
Oklahoma State University 431 Nancy Randolph Davis, Oklahoma State University, Stillwater, OK 74078	GPA: 3.59 SAT (ERW): 540-640 SAT (M): 520-640 ACT (C): 22-28 ED: No	Admit Rate: 67% Undergrad Enrollment: 20,323 Total Enrollment: 24,535	BS in Fashion Merchandising, emphases: Buying and Planning Visual Merchandising Degrees Awarded in the Program(s) (2020): N/A	Portfolio: Not req. Interview: Not req.
University of South Carolina 1705 College Street, Columbia, SC 29208	GPA: 3.53 SAT (ERW): 580-670 SAT (M): 560-670 ACT (C): 25-31 ED: No	Admit Rate: 68% Undergrad Enrollment: 27,271 Total Enrollment: 35,470	BS in Retailing, emphases: Retail Management Fashion Merchandising and Digital Innovations Degrees Awarded in the Program(s) (2020): 166	Portfolio: Not req. Interview: Not req.
Baylor University 1311 S 5th St, Waco, TX 76706	GPA: N/A SAT (ERW): 600-680 SAT (M): 590-680 ACT (C): 26-31 ED: Yes	Admit Rate: 68% Undergrad Enrollment: 14,399 Total Enrollment: 19,297	BS in Apparel Merchandising Degrees Awarded in the Program(s) (2020): 28	Portfolio: Not req. Interview: Not req.

SOUTH

School	Avg. GPA, SAT Evidence-Based Reading Writing (ERW), SAT Math (M), and ACT Composite (C) Early Decision (ED): Yes/No	Admission Statistics	Program(s)	Portfolio and/or Interview Required (Req.)
Southern Methodist University (SMU) 6425 Boaz Lane, Dallas, TX 75205	GPA: 3.64 SAT (ERW): 640-720 SAT (M): 660-760 ACT (C): 29-33 ED: Yes	Admit Rate: 53% Undergrad Enrollment: 6,827 Total Enrollment: 12,373	BA in Fashion Media Degrees Awarded in the Program(s) (2020): N/A	Portfolio: Not req. Interview: Not req.
Texas Tech University 2500 Broadway Lubbock, TX 79409	GPA: 3.63 SAT (ERW): 540-620 SAT (M): 530-620 ACT (C): 22-27 ED: No	Admit Rate: 70% Undergrad Enrollment: 33,269 Total Enrollment: 40,322	BS in Retail Management Degrees Awarded in the Program(s) (2020): 29	Portfolio: Not req. Interview: Not req.

School	Avg. GPA, SAT Evidence-Based Reading Writing (ERW), SAT Math (M), and ACT Composite (C) Early Decision (ED): Yes/No	Admission Statistics	Program(s)	Portfolio and/or Interview Required (Req.)
Texas Woman's University Old Main Building 415, P.O. Box 425529, Denton, TX 76204-5529	GPA: 3.17 SAT (ERW): 480-580 SAT (M): 460-560 ACT (C): 16-22 ED: No	Admit Rate: 94% Undergrad Enrollment: 10,664 Total Enrollment: 16,433	BS in Fashion Merchandising, emphases: Management Planning BS in Fashion Merchandising and BBA in Business Administration BS in Fashion Merchandising and BBA in Management BS in Fashion Merchandising and BBA in Marketing Degrees Awarded in the Program(s) (2020): 19	Portfolio: Not req. Interview: Not req.
University of North Texas Chilton Hall 331, 410 S. Avenue C, Denton, TX 76201	GPA: N/A SAT (ERW): 530-630 SAT (M): 520-610 ACT (C): ED: No	Admit Rate: 84% Undergrad Enrollment: 32,814 Total Enrollment: 40,953	BS in Merchandising Degrees Awarded in the Program(s) (2020): N/A	Portfolio: Not req. Interview: Not req.

SOUTH

School	Avg. GPA, SAT Evidence-Based Reading Writing (ERW), SAT Math (M), and ACT Composite (C) Early Decision (ED): Yes/No	Admission Statistics	Program(s)	Portfolio and/ or Interview Required (Req.)
University of Texas, Austin (UT Austin) 200 W 24th Street, Stop A2700, Austin, Texas 78712-1247	GPA: N/A SAT (ERW): 610-720 SAT (M): 600-750 ACT (C): 26-33 ED: No	Admit Rate: 32% Undergrad Enrollment: 40,048 Total Enrollment: 50,476	BS in Textiles and Apparel, option: Merchandising and Consumer Sciences Degrees Awarded in the Program(s) (2020): 54	Portfolio: Not req. Interview: Not req.
University of the Incarnate Word 4301 Broadway, San Antonio, TX 78209	GPA: 3.56 SAT (ERW): 480-580 SAT (M): 470-560 ACT (C): 17-23 ED: No	Admit Rate: 97% Undergrad Enrollment: 5,081 Total Enrollment: 7,917	BS in Fashion Management, concentration: Merchandising Degrees Awarded in the Program(s) (2020): 7	Portfolio: Not req. Interview: Not req.
Virginia Commonwealth University Virginia Commonwealth University, Richmond, VA 23284	GPA: 3.72 SAT (ERW): 540-640 SAT (M): 520-610 ACT (C): 21-28 ED: No	Admit Rate: 91% Undergrad Enrollment: 21,943 Total Enrollment: 29,070	BA in Fashion, concentration: Fashion Merchandising BA in Fashion, concentration: Fashion Merchandising and MS in Business, concentration: Marketing Management (4+1 Program) Degrees Awarded in the Program(s) (2020): 75	Portfolio: Not req. Interview: Not req.

School	Avg. GPA, SAT Evidence-Based Reading Writing (ERW), SAT Math (M), and ACT Composite (C) Early Decision (ED): Yes/No	Admission Statistics	Program(s)	Portfolio and/or Interview Required (Req.)
Virginia Tech University Virginia Polytechnic Institute and State University, Blacksburg, VA 24061	GPA: 3.96 SAT (ERW): 590-680 SAT (M): 580-690 ACT (C): 25-31 ED: Yes	Admit Rate: 66% Undergrad Enrollment: 30,020 Total Enrollment: 37,024	BS in Design and Merchandising, emphasis: Apparel Merchandising Degrees Awarded in the Program(s) (2020): N/A	Portfolio: Not req. Interview: Not req.
West Virginia University 650 Price Street, Morgantown, WV 26505	GPA: N/A SAT (ERW): 520-620 SAT (M): 510-610 ACT (C): 21-27 ED: No	Admit Rate: 84% Undergrad Enrollment: 20,495 Total Enrollment: 26,269	BS in Design and Merchandising, emphasis: Fashion Merchandising Degrees Awarded in the Program(s) (2020): N/A	Portfolio: Not req. Interview: Not req.

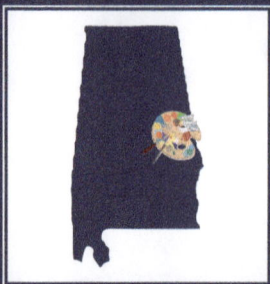

ALABAMA

ARKANSAS

DELAWARE

DISTRICT OF
COLUMBIA

FLORIDA

GEORGIA

KENTUCKY

LOUISIANA

MARYLAND

MISSISSIPPI

NORTH CAROLINA

OKLAHOMA

SOUTH CAROLINA

TENNESSEE

TEXAS

VIRGINIA

WEST VIRGINIA

AUBURN UNIVERSITY

Address: 210 Spidle Hall, Auburn, AL 36849
Website: http://humsci.auburn.edu/apparel/index.php
Contact: http://www.auburn.edu/enrollment/contact_us.php
Request for Information: https://apply.auburn.edu/register/inquiryform
Phone: (334) 844-4084
Email: ulricpv@auburn.edu

COST OF ATTENDANCE:

In-State Tuition & Fees: $11,796 | **Additional Expenses:** $21,648
Total: $33,444

Out-of-State Tuition & Fees: $31,956 | **Additional Expenses:** $21,648
Total: $53,604

Financial Aid: http://www.auburn.edu/administration/business-finance/finaid/

ADDITIONAL INFORMATION:

Available Degree(s)

- BS in Apparel Merchandising, Design, and Production Management, options in:
  - Merchandising
  - Apparel Design and Production Management

Freshman Portfolio Requirement

There is no portfolio requirement.

Scholarships Offered

Applicants are eligible for merit-based and achievement scholarships. Non-resident scholarships are up to $16,500 and resident scholarships go up to $10,500. Auburn University also awards general scholarships and department scholarships. For more information, visit: http://www.auburn.edu/scholarship/undergraduate/freshman.php

The College of Human Sciences offers College and Departmental Scholarships. For more information, visit: http://humsci.auburn.edu/academics/scholarships.php

Special Opportunities

According to Auburn University, "the Joseph S. Bruno Auburn Abroad in Italy program is strongly encouraged for apparel merchandising, design, and production management majors." The 12-week term is set in Ariccia, a small town near Rome. Students may earn their International Minor in Human Sciences while abroad. For more information, visit: http://www.humsci.auburn.edu/italy/index.php

An accelerated BS/MS program is available for Consumer and Design Sciences. For more information, visit: http://humsci.auburn.edu/cadsgrad/accelerated.php

UNIVERSITY OF DELAWARE

Address: 211 Alison Hall West, University of Delaware, Newark, DE 19716
Website: https://www.fashion.udel.edu/
Contact: https://www.fashion.udel.edu/about-us/contact-us
Request for Information: N/A
Phone: (302) 831-8714
Email: fashion-studies@udel.edu

COST OF ATTENDANCE:

In-State Tuition & Fees: $14,948 | **Additional Expenses:** $17,542
Total: $32,490

Out-of-State Tuition & Fees: $36,880 | **Additional Expenses:** $17,562
Total: $54,442

Financial Aid: https://www.udel.edu/students/student-financial-services/

ADDITIONAL INFORMATION:

Available Degree(s)

- BS in Fashion Merchandising and Management

Freshman Portfolio Requirement

There is no portfolio requirement.

Scholarships Offered

Merit scholarships, need-based grants, and endowed scholarships are available at UDel. Merit scholarships for in-state students range from 1,000-6,000 per year. Merit scholarships for out-of-state students range from 2,000-17,000 per year.For more information, visit: https://www.udel.edu/apply/undergraduate-admissions/financing-your-degree/

Special Opportunities

The Department of Fashion and Apparel Studies has opportunities for students to travel with faculty for one month during the winter session. Past locations have included Hong Kong (Internship), Paris, and Italy. Students may also travel domestically in the form of short field trips in New York City, Philadelphia, Washington, D.C., and California.

Notable Alumni

- Alyssa Dellureficio: Director of Store Planning & Space Planning at Party City
- Marielle Newman: Senior Manager of Color + Print innovation at Under Armour
- Ashley Paintsil: Fashion Journalism Professor at the University of Delaware

ALABAMA

ARKANSAS

DELAWARE

DISTRICT OF COLUMBIA

FLORIDA

GEORGIA

KENTUCKY

LOUISIANA

MARYLAND

MISSISSIPPI

NORTH CAROLINA

OKLAHOMA

SOUTH CAROLINA

TENNESSEE

TEXAS

VIRGINIA

WEST VIRGINIA

SOUTH

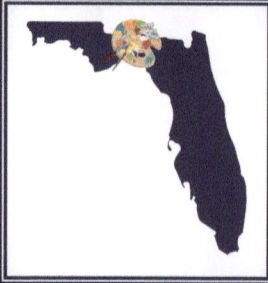

ALABAMA

ARKANSAS

DELAWARE

DISTRICT OF
COLUMBIA

FLORIDA

GEORGIA

KENTUCKY

LOUISIANA

MARYLAND

MISSISSIPPI

NORTH CAROLINA

OKLAHOMA

SOUTH CAROLINA

TENNESSEE

TEXAS

VIRGINIA

WEST VIRGINIA

FLORIDA STATE UNIVERSITY

Address: 540 W. Call Street, 239 Fine Arts Building, Tallahassee, FL 32306
Website: https://jimmorancollege.fsu.edu/academics/advising/retail-ent/
Contact: https://theatre.fsu.edu/about/contact/
Request for Information: https://connect.fsu.edu/register/uginforequest
Phone: (850) 644-6200
Email: admissions@fsu.edu

COST OF ATTENDANCE:

In-State Tuition & Fees: $5,666 | **Additional Expenses:** $17,820
Total: $23,486

Out-of-State Tuition & Fees: $18,796 | **Additional Expenses:** $18,936
Total: $37,732

Financial Aid: https://admissions.fsu.edu/freshman/finances/

ADDITIONAL INFORMATION:

Available Degree(s)

- BS in Retail Entrepreneurship, tracks:
  o Retail Merchandising
  o Product Development

Freshman Portfolio Requirement

There is no portfolio requirement.

Scholarships Offered

All students are automatically considered for Admission Scholarships. The University Freshman Scholarship is merit-based and awards $2,400 per year. The Presidential Scholars award is open to students admitted into the Florida State University Honors Program and awards $31,200 over four years. For more information, visit: https://admissions.fsu.edu/freshman/scholarships/

The College of Entrepreneurship also offers numerous scholarships: https://jimmorancollege.fsu.edu/academics/scholarships/

Special Opportunities

The College of Entrepreneurship offers a Textiles and Apparel Entrepreneurship minor.

Notable Alumni

- Naomi Elizée: Market Editor at Vogue
- Sara Blakely: Founder of Spanx

MIAMI INTERNATIONAL UNIVERSITY OF ART & DESIGN

Address: 1501 Biscayne Blvd Suite 100, Miami, FL 33132
Website: https://www.artinstitutes.edu/miami/academics/fashion
Contact: https://www.artinstitutes.edu/miami/about/contact-us
Request for Information: https://www.artinstitutes.edu/miami/request-information
Phone: (800) 225-9023
Email: miuadmissions@aii.edu

COST OF ATTENDANCE:

Tuition & Fees: $17,698 | **Additional Expenses:** $13,998
Total: $31,696

Financial Aid: https://www.artinstitutes.edu/miami/tuition-aid/financial-aid

ADDITIONAL INFORMATION:

Available Degree(s)

- BA in Fashion Merchandising

Freshman Portfolio Requirement

There is no portfolio requirement.

Scholarships Offered

The Arts Institutes offers scholarships via competitions. Awards include the $1,000-$12,000 through the FCCLA Competitions and 50% of the program total through the High School Initiative Scholarship. For more information, visit: https://www.artinstitutes.edu/miami/tuition-aid/scholarships

Special Opportunities

Students study topics such as sketching/illustration, pattern-making and draping, computer-aided design, clothing design, and garment construction.

Notable Alumni

- Jocelyn Altamiranda: Americas Regional Category Manager of Beauty at Dufry Group
- Damar Fairbanks: Senior Designer at Adidas
- Gustavo Alonso: Apparel Designer at Cintas

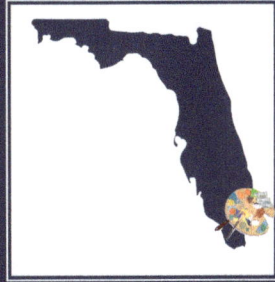

ALABAMA

ARKANSAS

DELAWARE

DISTRICT OF COLUMBIA

FLORIDA

GEORGIA

KENTUCKY

LOUISIANA

MARYLAND

MISSISSIPPI

NORTH CAROLINA

OKLAHOMA

SOUTH CAROLINA

TENNESSEE

TEXAS

VIRGINIA

WEST VIRGINIA

SOUTH

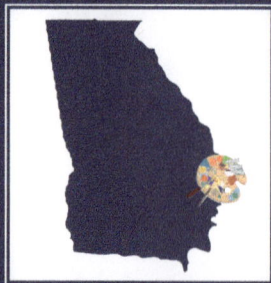

ALABAMA

ARKANSAS

DELAWARE

DISTRICT OF COLUMBIA

FLORIDA

GEORGIA

KENTUCKY

LOUISIANA

MARYLAND

MISSISSIPPI

NORTH CAROLINA

OKLAHOMA

SOUTH CAROLINA

TENNESSEE

TEXAS

VIRGINIA

WEST VIRGINIA

SAVANNAH COLLEGE OF ART & DESIGN (SCAD)

Address: 342 Bull St., Savannah, GA 31401
Website: https://www.fcs.uga.edu/tmi/fashion-merchandising
Contact: https://www.scad.edu/about/contact
Request for Information: https://admission.scad.edu/forms/reqInfo/rfi2
Phone: (912) 525-5100
Email: contact@scad.edu
Other locations: Atlanta, GA

COST OF ATTENDANCE:

Tuition & Fees: $38,340 | **Additional Expenses:** $15,269
Total: $53,609

Financial Aid: https://www.scad.edu/admission/financial-aid-and-scholarships

ADDITIONAL INFORMATION:

Available Degree(s)
- BFA in Fashion Marketing and Management

Freshman Portfolio Requirement
Applicants are not required to submit a portfolio. They are optional. However, portfolio submissions are required for achievement honors scholarship consideration.

- Submit via SlideRoom
- Portfolio may include a business or marketing plan, an identified challenge encountered in the market, and a proposal for a solution.
- Applicants are encouraged to collect the work in a multi-page PDF that includes branding, research, visuals, and writing. Applicants may also include a link to a 2-5 minute video presentation.
- To be considered for achievement honors scholarships, applicants must submit a resume/list of achievements as well

For more information, visit: https://www.scad.edu/admission/portfolio-and-writing-guidelines/undergraduate-portfolios

Scholarships Offered
All applicants including international students are eligible for merit-scholarships. The May and Paul Poetter Scholarship awards full tuition and is based on academic achievement. The Frances Larkin McCommon Scholarship awards full tuition and is based on artistic achievement. SCAD also offers SCAD academic scholarships ($1,500-$12,000). Among grands, the SCAD Athletic Grant awards $2,000-$12,000. For more information, visit: https://www.scad.edu/admission/financial-aid-and-scholarships

Furthermore, students may receive a scholarship award via the SCAD Challenge Scholarship. Awards range from $2,000-$4,000. For more information on this challenge, visit: https://www.scad.edu/admission/financial-aid-and-scholarships/scholarships/scad-challenge

Special Opportunities
High school students may earn college credits through joint enrollment and SCAD's Rising Star program as well as participate in SCAD Summer Seminars.

Fashion Marketing and Management students can study abroad in Japan.

SCAD offers a minor in Fashion Journalism.

UNIVERSITY OF GEORGIA

Address: Lamar Dodd School of Art, 270 River Road, Athens, GA 30602
Website: https://www.fcs.uga.edu/tmi/fashion-merchandising
Contact: https://reg.uga.edu/general-information/contact-us/
Request for Information: https://apply.uga.edu/register/?id=e6613431-a953-448d-97d3-8afa4e6b12ba
Phone: (706) 542-1511
Email: undergrad@admissions.uga.edu

COST OF ATTENDANCE:

In-State Tuition & Fees: $12,068 | **Additional Expenses:** $15,878
Total: $27,946

Out-of-State Tuition & Fees: $31,108 | **Additional Expenses:** $16,252
Total: $47,360

Financial Aid: https://osfa.uga.edu/

ADDITIONAL INFORMATION:

Available Degree(s)

- BS in Fashion Merchandising, emphasis: Fashion Brand Management

Freshman Portfolio Requirement

There is no portfolio requirement.

Scholarships Offered

The University of Georgia offers numerous academic-based, need-based, and both academic and need-based aids to students, many of which are open to Georgia residents, out-of-state students, and international students. Awards go as high as $22,900. For more information, visit: https://www.admissions.uga.edu/afford/scholarships/

Scholarships for Fashion Merchandising students are also available: https://www.fcs.uga.edu/tmi/scholarships-from-georgia-soft-goods

Special Opportunities

Fashion Merchandising students may participate in a 6-week summer program in London and a 3-week Maymester program in Ghana. Every other year, the students may also spend a semester in Cortona, Italy. For more information, visit: https://www.fcs.uga.edu/ssac/study-away

The College of Family and Consumer Sciences offers an Entrepreneurship Certificate.

Notable Alumni

- Amy Smilovic: Creator of the brand Tibi
- Maxine Kasselman Clark: Founder and Former CEO at Build-A-Bear Workshop
- Tim Mapes: Senior Vice President for Public Affairs at Delta Marketing

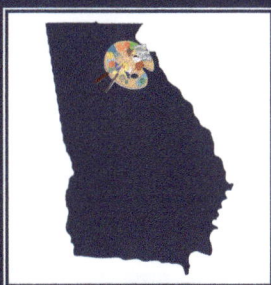

ALABAMA

ARKANSAS

DELAWARE

DISTRICT OF COLUMBIA

FLORIDA

GEORGIA

KENTUCKY

LOUISIANA

MARYLAND

MISSISSIPPI

NORTH CAROLINA

OKLAHOMA

SOUTH CAROLINA

TENNESSEE

TEXAS

VIRGINIA

WEST VIRGINIA

SOUTH

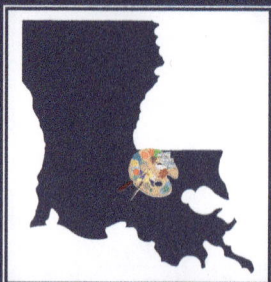

ALABAMA

ARKANSAS

DELAWARE

DISTRICT OF
COLUMBIA

FLORIDA

GEORGIA

KENTUCKY

LOUISIANA

MARYLAND

MISSISSIPPI

NORTH CAROLINA

OKLAHOMA

SOUTH CAROLINA

TENNESSEE

TEXAS

VIRGINIA

WEST VIRGINIA

LOUISIANA STATE UNIVERSITY (LSU)

Address: Louisiana State University, Baton Rouge, LA 70803
Website: https://www.lsu.edu/tam/
Contact: https://lsu.edu/about/requestinfo.php
Request for Information: https://www.lsu.edu/about/requestinfo.php
Phone: (225) 578-1175
Email: admissions@lsu.edu

COST OF ATTENDANCE:

In-State Tuition & Fees: $11,962 | **Additional Expenses:** $23,088
Total: $35,050

Out-of-State Tuition & Fees: $28,639 | **Additional Expenses:** $23,088
Total: $51,727

Financial Aid: https://www.lsu.edu/financialaid/index.php

ADDITIONAL INFORMATION:

Available Degree(s)

- BS in Textiles, Apparel, & Merchandising, concentration: Merchandising

Freshman Portfolio Requirement

There is no portfolio requirement.

Scholarships Offered

Louisiana State University offers merit-based scholarships, need-based awards, major-specific scholarships, the Stamps Scholarship, and more. Awards range from $500 to full cost of attendance. For more information, visit: https://www.lsu.edu/financialaid/types_of_scholarships/entering_freshman_scholarships/index.php

Special Opportunities

A component collection of the Louisiana Museum of Natural History at LSU, the Textile & Costume Museum holds items including apparel, accessories, household textiles, piece goods, books, patterns, and a variety of items related to textile and apparel production, use, and care.

The Department of Textiles, Apparel Design, and Merchandising houses numerous facilities including a sewing lab, 3D printing machine, apparel production lab, body scanning technology, a textile printer, and a textile science lab.

Notable Alumni

- Madi Meserole: Design Director at MEZ Atelier
- Chelsey Blankenship & Annie Claire Bass: Co-Founders of SoSis Boutique
- Natasha Miller Popich: Owner and Designer at Natasha Marie Bridal

NORTH CAROLINA STATE UNIVERSITY AT RALEIGH

Address: 1020 Main Campus Dr., Raleigh, NC 27606
Website: https://textiles.ncsu.edu/tatm/fashion-and-textile-management/
Contact: https://textiles.ncsu.edu/directory/people?group=textile-and-apparel-technology-and-management&compact=false
Request for Information: N/A
Phone: (919) 515-3442
Email: undergrad-admissions@ncsu.edu

COST OF ATTENDANCE:

In-State Tuition & Fees: $9,130 | **Additional Expenses:** $15,855
Total: $24,985

Out-of-State Tuition & Fees: $29,916 | **Additional Expenses:** $16,064
Total: $45,980

Financial Aid: https://studentservices.ncsu.edu/your-money/financial-aid/

ADDITIONAL INFORMATION:

Available Degree(s)

- BS in Fashion and Textile Management, concentrations:
  - Fashion Development and Product Management
  - Brand Management and Marketing

Freshman Portfolio Requirement

There is no portfolio requirement.

Scholarships Offered

NC State offers a number of Rising Freshmen Distinctive Scholarships. The Park Scholarship awards $116,000 to in-state students over four years and $208,000 to out-of-state students over four years. For more information, visit: https://studentservices.ncsu.edu/your-money/financial-aid/types/scholarships/

Every year, the College of Textiles awards up to 10 Centennial Scholarships ($15,000-$22,000 a year) and more than a 100 NCTF Distinguished Merit and Prestige scholarships. For more information, visit: https://textiles.ncsu.edu/admissions/scholarships/

Special Opportunities

Rising high school seniors are eligible to participate in the Summer Textile Exploration Program.

Fashion and Textile Management students may spend a semester in China, Italy, England, Czech Republic, or Australia. There are also summer programs in Italy, Germany, and Argentina. For more information, visit: https://textiles.ncsu.edu/about/international/study-abroad/international-exchange-students/

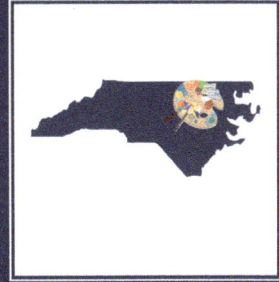

ALABAMA
ARKANSAS
DELAWARE
DISTRICT OF COLUMBIA
FLORIDA
GEORGIA
KENTUCKY
LOUISIANA
MARYLAND
MISSISSIPPI
NORTH CAROLINA
OKLAHOMA
SOUTH CAROLINA
TENNESSEE
TEXAS
VIRGINIA
WEST VIRGINIA

SOUTH

UNIVERSITY OF NORTH CAROLINA AT GREENSBORO

Address: 1400 Spring Garden St, Greensboro, NC 27402
Website: https://bryan.uncg.edu/programs/undergraduate/major/consumer-apparel-retail-studies/
Contact: https://bryan.uncg.edu/contact/
Request for Information: https://spartanlink.uncg.edu/register.asp
Phone: (336) 334-5000
Email: admissions@uncg.edu

COST OF ATTENDANCE:

In-State Tuition & Fees: $7,406 | **Additional Expenses:** $9,423
Total: $16,829

Out-of-State Tuition & Fees: $22,565 | **Additional Expenses:** $9,423
Total: $31,988

Financial Aid: https://admissions.uncg.edu/costs-aid/costs/

ADDITIONAL INFORMATION:

Available Degree(s)

- BS in Consumer, Apparel, and Retail Studies, concentration: Retailing and Consumer Studies

Freshman Portfolio Requirement

There is no portfolio requirement.

Scholarships Offered

UNCG offers incoming freshmen merit-based scholarships. The Blue and Gold Scholarships range in value and duration. Students must submit a 250- to 500-word essay in addition to their application. The Chancellor and Spartan Scholarships are both need-based and merit-based. For more information, visit: https://admissions.uncg.edu/costs-aid/scholarships/

The School of Business and Economics awards a number of scholarships each year, majority of which are need-based. For more information, visit: https://bryan.uncg.edu/current-students/forms/apply-for-scholarships/

Special Opportunities

Consumer, Apparel, and Retail Studies students may spend a summer, a semester, or a year in China, Italy, England, Australia, New Zealand, and Botswana. For more information, visit: https://docs.google.com/document/d/1zPb971SJ_DkMAnjbmsQY-ipnVYKyzma8DpiadHfkE_U/edit

UNCG offers an Accelerated Master's Program that allows students to earn a MS in Retail Studies in 12-18 months after receiving their undergraduate degree. For more information, visit: https://bryan.uncg.edu/programs/masters/list/consumer-apparel-and-retail-studies-accelerated-masters-program/

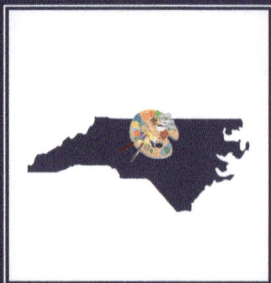

ALABAMA
ARKANSAS
DELAWARE
DISTRICT OF COLUMBIA
FLORIDA
GEORGIA
KENTUCKY
LOUISIANA
MARYLAND
MISSISSIPPI
NORTH CAROLINA
OKLAHOMA
SOUTH CAROLINA
TENNESSEE
TEXAS
VIRGINIA
WEST VIRGINIA

OKLAHOMA STATE UNIVERSITY

Address: Oklahoma State University, Stillwater, OK 74078
Website: https://go.okstate.edu/undergraduate-academics/majors/fashion-merchandising.html
Contact: https://go.okstate.edu/admissions/contact-us.html
Request for Information: N/A
Phone: (405) 744-5358
Email: admissions@okstate.edu

COST OF ATTENDANCE:

In-State Tuition & Fees: $13,920 | **Additional Expenses:** $11,000
Total: $24,920

Out-of-State Tuition & Fees: $29,440 | **Additional Expenses:** $11,000
Total: $40,440

Financial Aid: https://go.okstate.edu/scholarships-financial-aid/

ADDITIONAL INFORMATION:

Available Degree(s)

- BS in Fashion Merchandising, emphases:
  o Buying and Planning
  o Visual Merchandising

Freshman Portfolio Requirement

There is no portfolio requirement.

Scholarships Offered

Students are automatically considered for scholarships when they apply for admission. Most scholarships are merit-based. There are a variety of in-state and out-of-state scholarships. Awards vary from $1,000 per year (based on GPA and ACT/SAT) to partnered scholarships that may cover full tuition for five years (Oklahoma's Promise). For more information, visit: https://go.okstate.edu/scholarships-financial-aid/types-of-aid/scholarships-and-grants/freshman-scholarships/index.html

Special Opportunities

Students may attend the annual trip to New York to meet alumni and interview at prospective internship locations. Additionally, there are faculty-led study abroad summer experiences where students may earn course credit in locations such as Paris, Spain, and London.

Notable Alumni

- Ali Barbera: Senior Director of Product Development at Calvin Klein
- Rachel Green: Merchandising Manager at Sport Obermeyer
- Toby Hanyok: Associate Vendor Manager and Buyer at Woot

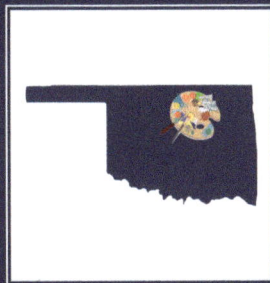

ALABAMA
ARKANSAS
DELAWARE
DISTRICT OF COLUMBIA
FLORIDA
GEORGIA
KENTUCKY
LOUISIANA
MARYLAND
MISSISSIPPI
NORTH CAROLINA
OKLAHOMA
SOUTH CAROLINA
TENNESSEE
TEXAS
VIRGINIA
WEST VIRGINIA

SOUTH

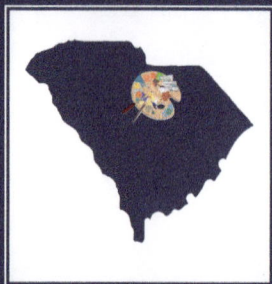

UNIVERSITY OF SOUTH CAROLINA

Address: 1705 College Street, Columbia, SC 29208
Website: https://sc.edu/study/colleges_schools/hrsm/study/areasofstudy/retl/
Contact: https://www.sc.edu/about/contact/
Request for Information: https://apply.sc.edu/register/web
Phone: (803) 777-7700
Email: admissions-ugrad@sc.edu

COST OF ATTENDANCE:

In-State Tuition & Fees: $12,228 | **Additional Expenses:** $21,674
Total: $33,902

Out-of-State Tuition & Fees: $33,528 | **Additional Expenses:** $21,621
Total: $55,149

Financial Aid: https://sc.edu/about/offices_and_divisions/financial_aid/index.php

ADDITIONAL INFORMATION:

Available Degree(s)

- BS in Retailing, emphases:
  o Retail Management
  o Fashion Merchandising and Digital Innovations

Freshman Portfolio Requirement

There is no portfolio requirement.

Scholarships Offered

University of South Carolina offers numerous merit scholarships. The Stamps Scholars program is open to both in-state students (up to $90,000 over four years) and out-of-state students ($191,000 over four years). In-state students are also eligible for the lottery-funded HOPE, LIFE and Palmetto Fellows Scholarships provided by the State of South Carolina. For more information, visit: https://www.sc.edu/about/offices_and_divisions/financial_aid/scholarships/index.php

Retailing majors may also take advantage of scholarships offered through the College of Hospitality, Retail, & Sports Management: https://sc.edu/financialaid/scholarshipmgmt/scholarshipprint.php

Special Opportunities

Retailing students can take Fashion and Retail in London and Paris during Maymester. The Department of Retailing sponsors selected students to attend the New York Fashion Week and has also brought students to the Retail's Big Show.

Notable Alumni

- Sophie Kerr-Dineen: Vice President of Growth and Strategy at ScienceMagic
- Melissa Karl: Vice President of Branding and Marketing at STONE AND STRAND
- Anna Hanley: Financial Planning and Merchandising Analyst at New Flag GmbH

ALABAMA

ARKANSAS

DELAWARE

DISTRICT OF COLUMBIA

FLORIDA

GEORGIA

KENTUCKY

LOUISIANA

MARYLAND

MISSISSIPPI

NORTH CAROLINA

OKLAHOMA

SOUTH CAROLINA

TENNESSEE

TEXAS

VIRGINIA

WEST VIRGINIA

BAYLOR UNIVERSITY

Address: 1311 S 5th St, Waco, TX 76706
Website: https://www.baylor.edu/admissions/index.php?id=872542
Contact: https://www.baylor.edu/admissions/index.php?id=871966
Request for Information: N/A
Phone: (254) 710-3436
Email: admissions@baylor.edu

COST OF ATTENDANCE:

Tuition & Fees: $50,232 | **Additional Expenses:** $12,682
Total: $62,914

Financial Aid: https://www.baylor.edu/admissions/index.php?id=871964

ADDITIONAL INFORMATION:

Available Degree(s)

- BS in Apparel Merchandising

Freshman Portfolio Requirement

There is no portfolio requirement.

Scholarships Offered

All applicants are automatically considered for scholarships based on their high school academic performance, including students who apply as test optional. The Carr P. Collins Scholars Program awards a minimum of $5,750 per year to recipients. Students in the Honors College may have additional scholarship opportunities. For more information, visit: https://www.baylor.edu/admissions/index.php?id=873057

The Family & Consumer Sciences Department offers scholarships to current undergraduates. All of these scholarships are based on merit, and some are also need-based. Seniors or Junior. For more information, visit: https://www.baylor.edu/fcs/index.php?id=947273

Special Opportunities

Apparel Merchandising students must complete an internship as part of their degree requirements. The Spring Fashion Show offers students an opportunity to oversee public relations, ticket sales, programs and training of models.

Apparel Merchandising students are encouraged to participate in the Apparel Studies European Tour over the summer.

Notable Alumni

- Jessica Chia: Director of Beauty Brands Strategy at Intrepid Investment Bankers
- Carol McColgin: Fashion & Beauty Director at The Hollywood Reporter

ALABAMA
ARKANSAS
DELAWARE
DISTRICT OF COLUMBIA
FLORIDA
GEORGIA
KENTUCKY
LOUISIANA
MARYLAND
MISSISSIPPI
NORTH CAROLINA
OKLAHOMA
SOUTH CAROLINA
TENNESSEE
TEXAS
VIRGINIA
WEST VIRGINIA

SOUTH

ALABAMA

ARKANSAS

DELAWARE

DISTRICT OF
COLUMBIA

FLORIDA

GEORGIA

KENTUCKY

LOUISIANA

MARYLAND

MISSISSIPPI

NORTH CAROLINA

OKLAHOMA

SOUTH CAROLINA

TENNESSEE

TEXAS

VIRGINIA

WEST VIRGINIA

SOUTHERN METHODIST UNIVERSITY (SMU)

Address: 6425 Boaz Lane, Dallas, TX 75205
Website: https://www.smu.edu/Meadows/AreasOfStudy/
Journalism/UndergraduateStudies/FashionMediaBA
Contact: https://www.smu.edu/Meadows/About/Contact
Request for Information: https://admission.smu.edu/register/info
Phone: 214-768-2000
Email: meadowsadmission@smu.edu

COST OF ATTENDANCE:

Tuition & Fees: $60,236 | **Additional Expenses:** $20,914
Total: $81,150

Financial Aid: https://www.smu.edu/EnrollmentServices/
financialaid

ADDITIONAL INFORMATION:

Available Degree(s)

- BA in Fashion Media

Freshman Portfolio Requirement

There is no portfolio requirement.

Scholarships Offered

SMU offers several scholarship opportunities to students, including
the President's Scholar Award (full tuition and fees for up to 8
semesters), the SMU Distinguished Scholarship (maximum $25,000
per year for four years), and the Second Century Scholars ($20,000
per year for four years), among many others. For more information,
visit: https://www.smu.edu/EnrollmentServices/financialaid/
TypesOfAid/Scholarships

The School of the Arts offers a number of scholarships: https://
www.smu.edu/Meadows/Admissions/Undergraduate/FinancialAid

Special Opportunities

SMU's Journalism Complex houses cutting-edge computer
equipment, a broadcast studio, and a convergence newsroom. It
is open to journalism majors 24/7. In addition, classes never have
more than 15 students, meaning more interaction with professors.

TEXAS TECH UNIVERSITY

Address: 2500 Broadway Lubbock, TX 79409
Website: https://www.depts.ttu.edu/hs/hrm/ret/index.php
Contact: https://www.ttu.edu/about/contact.php
Request for Information: Press "Request More Information" -
https://www.depts.ttu.edu/hs/prospective_students/fashion/
apparel_design.php
Phone: (806) 742-2011
Email: admissions@ttu.edu

COST OF ATTENDANCE:

In-State Tuition & Fees: $11,600 | **Additional Expenses:** $15,556
Total: $27,156

Out-of-State Tuition & Fees: $23,870 | **Additional Expenses:** $15,556
Total: $39,426

Financial Aid: http://www.depts.ttu.edu/financialaid/

ADDITIONAL INFORMATION:

Available Degree(s)

- BS in Retail Management, concentrations: Fashion
  Merchandising

Freshman Portfolio Requirement

There is no portfolio requirement.

Scholarships Offered

Applicants are automatically considered for general scholarships.
Students who apply test-optional will be evaluated holistically.
TTU's Presidential Merit Scholarships range in value from $1,000-
$9,000 per year. Additionally, National Merit Finalists may receive
full cost of attendance. For more information, visit: https://www.
depts.ttu.edu/scholarships/incFreshman.php

Special Opportunities

Retail Management students will have the opportunity to organize
an annual retail symposium and retail reception.

Notable Alumni

- Kim Tuttle: Co-Founder of Motherputter
- Catherine Carter: Director of Merchandising at Gap
- Kelley Brandt: Women and Children's Apparel Buyer at Dallas
  Cowboys

ALABAMA
ARKANSAS
DELAWARE
DISTRICT OF
COLUMBIA
FLORIDA
GEORGIA
KENTUCKY
LOUISIANA
MARYLAND
MISSISSIPPI
NORTH CAROLINA
OKLAHOMA
SOUTH CAROLINA
TENNESSEE
TEXAS
VIRGINIA
WEST VIRGINIA

SOUTH

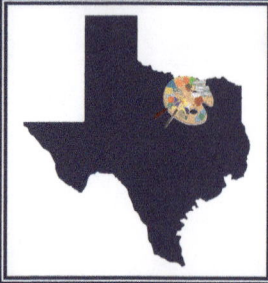

ALABAMA

ARKANSAS

DELAWARE

DISTRICT OF COLUMBIA

FLORIDA

GEORGIA

KENTUCKY

LOUISIANA

MARYLAND

MISSISSIPPI

NORTH CAROLINA

OKLAHOMA

SOUTH CAROLINA

TENNESSEE

TEXAS

VIRGINIA

WEST VIRGINIA

TEXAS WOMAN'S UNIVERSITY

Address: 304 Administration Dr, Denton, TX 76204
Website: https://twu.edu/fashion/
Contact: https://twu.edu/contact-twu/
Request for Information: https://twu.edu/admissions/info-request/
Phone: (866) 809-6130
Email: admissions@twu.edu

COST OF ATTENDANCE:

In-State Tuition & Fees: $9,960 | **Additional Expenses:** $14,586
Total: $24,546

Out-of-State Tuition & Fees: $22,230 | **Additional Expenses:** $14,586
Total: $36,816

Financial Aid: https://twu.edu/finaid/

ADDITIONAL INFORMATION:

Available Degree(s)

- BS in Fashion Merchandising, emphases:
  o Management
  o Planning
- BS in Fashion Merchandising and BBA in Business Administration
- BS in Fashion Merchandising and BBA in Management
- BS in Fashion Merchandising and BBA in Marketing

Freshman Portfolio Requirement

There is no portfolio requirement.

Scholarships Offered

Scholarships offered at TWU are need-based and/or merit-based and vary in award amounts. Additionally, fashion students may be eligible for Fashion and Textiles scholarships. Students must apply separately to these awards. For more information, visit: https://twu.edu/fashion/scholarships/

Special Opportunities

High school students aged 9-18 are eligible to attend TWU's summer Fashion Camps and listen to feature faculty members, graduate students, and industry professionals.

Notable Alumni

- Carla Robertson: Designer, Sewing Educator, and Owner of C. Adele Creations
- Joyce Yeboah Ababio: Fashion Designer and President of Joyce Ababio College of Creative Design
- Doze Butler: Associate Dean for the School of Agriculture, Fisheries and Human Sciences at the University of Arkansas at Pine Bluff

UNIVERSITY OF NORTH TEXAS

Address: 1201 W. Mulberry St., Denton, TX 76201
Website: https://cmht.unt.edu/bachelor-science-merchandising
Contact: https://admissions.unt.edu/contact-us
Request for Information: https://admissions.unt.edu/requestinfo
Phone: (940) 565-2855
Email: cvad@unt.edu

COST OF ATTENDANCE:

In-State Tuition & Fees: $11,514 | **Additional Expenses:** $13,860
Total: $25,374

Out-of-State Tuition & Fees: $24,514 | **Additional Expenses: $13,860**
otal: $38,374

Financial Aid: https://financialaid.unt.edu/

ADDITIONAL INFORMATION:

Available Degree(s)

- BS in Merchandising

Freshman Portfolio Requirement

There is no portfolio requirement.

Scholarships Offered

Merit-based awards offered at University of North Texas include the UNT Excellence Scholarship ($1,000-$12,000) and the UNT Meritorious Scholarship for National Merit Finalists (full cost of attendance). Out-of-state and international students who receive UNT Excellence Scholarship are eligible for a Texas state competitive scholarship waiver for the difference between in-state and out-of-state tuition. For more information, visit: https://financialaid.unt.edu/freshmen-scholarships

The College of Merchandising, Hospitality & Tourism awards competitive scholarships to eligible students. For more information, visit: https://cmht.unt.edu/cmht-competitive-scholarship

Special Opportunities

Students have access to the Texas Fashion Collection, housing over 20,000 articles of historic clothing and accessories as well as more than 40,000 images. For more information, visit: https://tfc.cvad.unt.edu/

The Merchandising and Digital Retailing Department offers Merchandising students an immersion program in Europe and a study tour in New York City.

Notable Alumni

- Wende Zomnir: Co-Founder and Creative Director at Urban Decay
- Lanessa Elrod: President and CEO at Louis Vuitton Americas Zone
- Sam Moon: Owner of Sam Moon Trading Company

ALABAMA

ARKANSAS

DELAWARE

DISTRICT OF COLUMBIA

FLORIDA

GEORGIA

KENTUCKY

LOUISIANA

MARYLAND

MISSISSIPPI

NORTH CAROLINA

OKLAHOMA

SOUTH CAROLINA

TENNESSEE

TEXAS

VIRGINIA

WEST VIRGINIA

SOUTH

ALABAMA

ARKANSAS

DELAWARE

DISTRICT OF COLUMBIA

FLORIDA

GEORGIA

KENTUCKY

LOUISIANA

MARYLAND

MISSISSIPPI

NORTH CAROLINA

OKLAHOMA

SOUTH CAROLINA

TENNESSEE

TEXAS

VIRGINIA

WEST VIRGINIA

UNIVERSITY OF TEXAS, AUSTIN

Address: UT Austin, Austin, TX 78712
Website: https://he.utexas.edu/txa/academics/undergraduate-program#option-ii-merchandising-and-consumer-sciences
Contact: https://he.utexas.edu/about/contact
Request for Information: N/A
Phone: (512) 475-7399
Email: admissions@austin.utexas.edu

COST OF ATTENDANCE:

In-State Tuition & Fees: $10,824 | **Additional Expenses:** $16,904
Total: $27,728

Out-of-State Tuition & Fees: $38,326 | **Additional Expenses:** $16,904
Total: $55,230

Financial Aid: https://finaid.utexas.edu/

ADDITIONAL INFORMATION:

Available Degree(s)

- BS in Textiles and Apparel, option: Merchandising and Consumer Sciences

Freshman Portfolio Requirement

There is no portfolio requirement.

Scholarships Offered

Students are automatically considered for institutional aid. For more information, visit: https://admissions.utexas.edu/afford/undergrad-scholarships

The School of Human Ecology administrates various need and merit-based scholarships to continuing students. For more information, visit: https://he.utexas.edu/students/scholarships

Special Opportunities

Textiles and Apparel majors are eligible for the Departmental Honors program. For more information, visit: https://he.utexas.edu/txa/academics/undergraduate-program/honors

UT Austin hosts the Textiles and Apparel High School Challenge, where students must design an apparel or accessory using materials from the trash and winners receive tickets to the TXA Fashion Show and a private backstage tour. For more information, visit: https://he.utexas.edu/txa/academics/career-development/high-school-design-challenge

Apparel students can participate in a week-long NYC fashion program led by Iris Apfel. The French Fashion: History & Techniques. The Textiles and Apparel Program also offers French Fashion: History & Techniques, an immersive learning opportunity.

Notable Alumni

- Avani Patel: Director of Operations at Depop
- Viviana Martinez: Location Planning Analyst at Ross
- Javier Uriegas: Product Operations Analyst at Levi Strauss

UNIVERSITY OF THE INCARNATE WORD

Address: 4301 Broadway, San Antonio, TX 78209
Website: https://www.uiw.edu/smd/academics/undergraduate/
fashion-management/index.html
Contact: https://www.uiw.edu/contact/index.html
Request for Information: https://www.uiw.edu/gouiw/index.html
Phone: (210) 829-6005
Email: admis@uiwtx.edu

COST OF ATTENDANCE:

Tuition & Fees: $33,100 | **Additional Expenses:** $17,712
Total: $50,812

Financial Aid: https://www.uiw.edu/finaid/index.html

ADDITIONAL INFORMATION:

Available Degree(s)

- BS in Fashion Management, concentration: Merchandising

Freshman Portfolio Requirement

There is no portfolio requirement.

Scholarships Offered

Applicants are automatically considered for Freshman Academic
Scholarships based on high school GPA. These scholarships range
between $7,000 - $20,000 per year and are open to international
students. For more information, visit: https://www.uiw.edu/
admissions/scholarships.html

The Jurren Sullivan Center for Fashion Management awards
fashion students scholarships that range from $1,000 to
$2,675. For more information, visit: https://www.uiw.edu/smd/
students/scholarships.html

Special Opportunities

The Fashion Department offers a semester away program each
year and has taken students to New York, London, Paris, and Rome.
Students may also study at London College of Fashion.

ALABAMA

ARKANSAS

DELAWARE

DISTRICT OF
COLUMBIA

FLORIDA

GEORGIA

KENTUCKY

LOUISIANA

MARYLAND

MISSISSIPPI

NORTH CAROLINA

OKLAHOMA

SOUTH CAROLINA

TENNESSEE

TEXAS

VIRGINIA

WEST VIRGINIA

SOUTH

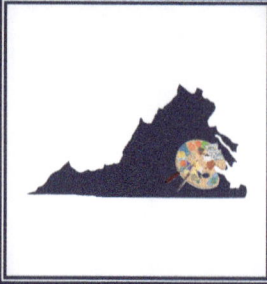

ALABAMA

ARKANSAS

DELAWARE

DISTRICT OF
COLUMBIA

FLORIDA

GEORGIA

KENTUCKY

LOUISIANA

MARYLAND

MISSISSIPPI

NORTH CAROLINA

OKLAHOMA

SOUTH CAROLINA

TENNESSEE

TEXAS

VIRGINIA

WEST VIRGINIA

VIRGINIA COMMONWEALTH UNIVERSITY

Address: Virginia Commonwealth University, Richmond, VA 23284
Website: https://arts.vcu.edu/academics/departments/fashion/fashion-merchandising-ba/
Contact: https://www.vcu.edu/contacts/
Request for Information: https://www.vcu.edu/admissions/contact-admissions/ugrad-interest-form/
Phone: (804) 828-0100
Email: ugrad@vcu.edu

COST OF ATTENDANCE:

In-State Tuition & Fees: $17,140 | **Additional Expenses:** $17,549
Total: $34,689

Out-of-State Tuition & Fees: $38,478 | **Additional Expenses:** $17,549
Total: $56,027

Financial Aid: https://finaid.vcu.edu/

ADDITIONAL INFORMATION:

Available Degree(s)

- BA in Fashion, concentration: Fashion Merchandising
- BA in Fashion, concentration: Fashion Merchandising and MS in Business, concentration: Marketing Management (4+1 Program)

Freshman Portfolio Requirement

There is no portfolio requirement.

Scholarships Offered

First-year students are automatically considered for VCUarts talent scholarships ($5,000-$12,000 annually) based on academic merit and artistic talent. University scholarship awards vary based on the scholarship, but range from $8,000 per year to $16,000 plus room and board per year. For more information, visit: https://arts.vcu.edu/admissions/scholarships/

Special Opportunities

VCUarts Qatar is the sister campus located in Doha, Qatar. Fashion design and merchandising students may apply to spend a semester at this campus. Additionally, students may study abroad over the summer at the Santa Reparata International School of Art in Florence, Italy or spend a semester at the University of Westminster in London. For more information, visit: https://arts.vcu.edu/academics/departments/fashion/study-abroad-fashion/

Notable Alumni

- Tiffany Mariner: Director of Merchandise Execution at Macy's
- Victoria Long: Manager of Operations and Visual Merchandising at Macy's

VIRGINIA POLYTECHNIC INSTITUTE AND STATE UNIVERSITY (VIRGINIA TECH)

Address: Virginia Polytechnic Institute and State University, Blacksburg, VA 24061
Website: https://liberalarts.vt.edu/academics/majors-and-minors/fashion-merchandising-and-design.html
Contact: https://vt.edu/contacts.html
Request for Information: https://vt.edu/admissions/forms/inquiry1.html
Phone: (540) 231-6267
Email: admissions@vt.edu

COST OF ATTENDANCE:

In-State Tuition & Fees: $14,175 | **Additional Expenses:** $9,876
Total: $24,051

Out-of-State Tuition & Fees: $33,857 | **Additional Expenses:** $9,876
Total: $43,733

Financial Aid: https://vt.edu/admissions/undergraduate/cost.html

ADDITIONAL INFORMATION:

Available Degree(s)

- BS in Fashion Merchandising and Design, specialization: Apparel Merchandising

Freshman Portfolio Requirement

There is no portfolio requirement.

Scholarships Offered

All first-time students are automatically considered for the Virginia Tech Scholars Scholarship program. General Scholarships awards typically range from $1000 to $3000. Students who are accepted to the Honors College are eligible for additional funding. For more information, visit: https://liberalarts.vt.edu/beyond-the-classroom/scholarships-and-awards.html

The Department of Apparel, Housing, and Resource Management also offers program-specific scholarships to Fashion Merchandising and Design students. For more information, visit: https://liberalarts.vt.edu/beyond-the-classroom/scholarships-and-awards/ahrm-scholarships.html

Special Opportunities

Students may network with fashion retailers and merchandisers through the week-long New York Fashion Study Tour. The European Study Abroad is offered every other summer and involves visits with universities, design houses, and European boutiques in London, Paris, Rome, Florence, and other fashion capitals. For more information, visit: https://liberalarts.vt.edu/departments-and-schools/apparel-housing-and-resource-management/why-study/study-abroad.html

ALABAMA
ARKANSAS
DELAWARE
DISTRICT OF COLUMBIA
FLORIDA
GEORGIA
KENTUCKY
LOUISIANA
MARYLAND
MISSISSIPPI
NORTH CAROLINA
OKLAHOMA
SOUTH CAROLINA
TENNESSEE
TEXAS
VIRGINIA
WEST VIRGINIA

SOUTH

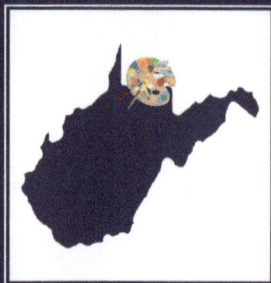

ALABAMA

ARKANSAS

DELAWARE

DISTRICT OF
COLUMBIA

FLORIDA

GEORGIA

KENTUCKY

LOUISIANA

MARYLAND

MISSISSIPPI

NORTH CAROLINA

OKLAHOMA

SOUTH CAROLINA

TENNESSEE

TEXAS

VIRGINIA

WEST VIRGINIA

WEST VIRGINIA UNIVERSITY

Address: 650 Price Street, Morgantown, WV 26505
Website: https://admissions.wvu.edu/academics/majors/fashion-dress-and-merchandising
Contact: https://admissions.wvu.edu/contact-us
Request for Information: https://admissions.wvu.edu/request-information
Phone: (304) 293-2121
Email: https://admissions.wvu.edu/admissions-counselors#anchor-counselorftf

COST OF ATTENDANCE:

In-State Tuition & Fees: $9,816 | **Additional Expenses:** $14,648
Total: $24,464

Out-of-State Tuition & Fees: $26,664 | **Additional Expenses:** $15,148
Total: $41,812

Financial Aid: https://financialaid.wvu.edu/applying-for-aid

ADDITIONAL INFORMATION:

Available Degree(s)

- BS in Design and Merchandising, emphasis: Fashion Merchandising

Freshman Portfolio Requirement

There is no portfolio requirement.

Scholarships Offered

All first-time students including international applicants are automatically considered for merit scholarships. Scholarship of Distinction for in-state score senders range between $1,250-$4,000 and out-of-state score senders range between $7,000-$16,000. Go First Scholarship The Go First Scholarship is for test optional applicants. The Davis College of Agriculture, Natural Resources and Design offers additional merit-based scholarships based on GPA and SAT/ACT test score. For more information, visit: https://admissions.wvu.edu/cost-and-aid/scholarship-chart

Special Opportunities

Fashion, Dress and Merchandising students may take advantage of a four-week, six-credit summer program in Tuscany and Milan, Italy. There is also a four-credit, 16-day summer program in Czech Republic and Austria.

Notable Alumni

- Nesha Sanghavi: CEO at UG Apparel & chicka-d

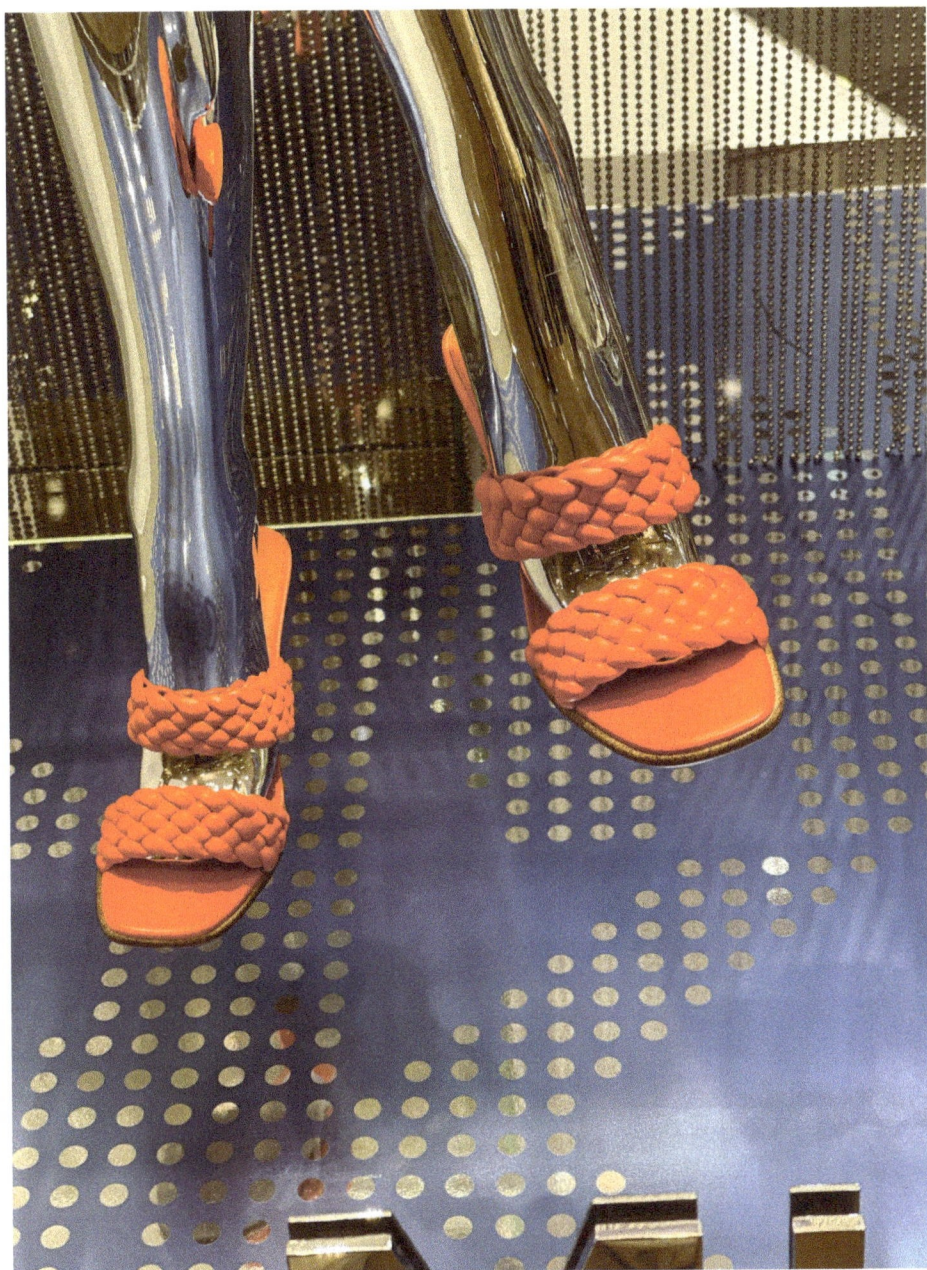

ALASKA

ARIZONA

CALIFORNIA

COLORADO

HAWAII

IDAHO

MONTANA

NEVADA

NEW MEXICO

OREGON

UTAH

WASHINGTON

WYOMING

CHAPTER 14

REGION FOUR

WEST

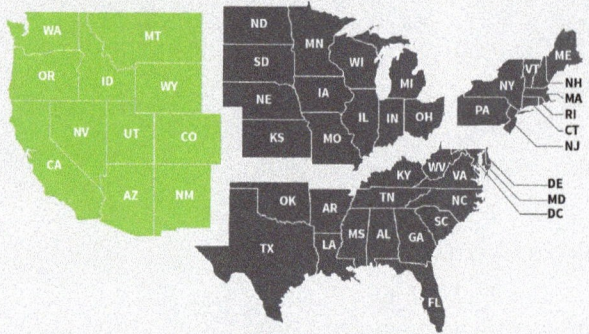

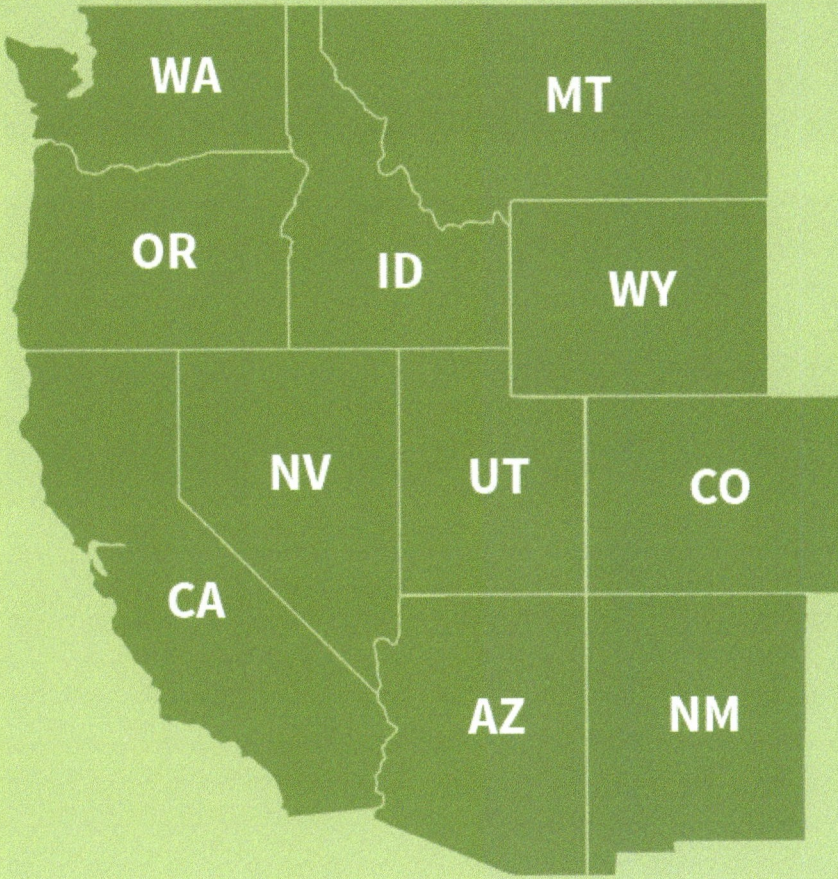

10 Programs | 13 States

1. CA - Academy of Art University
2. CA - California State Polytechnic University, Pomona (CalPoly Pomona)
3. CA - California State University, Long Beach (CSULB)
4. CA - California State University, Northridge (CSUN)
5. CA - Fashion Institute of Design and Merchandising (FIDM)
6. CA - San Francisco State University
7. CO - Colorado State University, Ft. Collins
8. HI - University of Hawaii at Manoa
9. OR - Oregon State University
10. WA - Washington State University

FASHION MERCHANDISING PROGRAMS

School	Avg. GPA, SAT Evidence-Based Reading Writing (ERW), SAT Math (M), and ACT Composite (C) Early Decision (ED): Yes/No	Admission Statistics	Program(s)	Portfolio and/or Interview Required (Req.)
Academy of Art University 79 New Montgomery St., San Francisco, CA 94105	GPA: N/A SAT (ERW): N/A SAT (M): N/A ACT (C): N/A *Academy of Art has an open admissions policy. ED: No	Admit Rate: N/A Undergrad Enrollment: 6,124 Total Enrollment: 8,928	BA in Fashion Journalism BFA in Fashion Marketing BFA in Fashion Merchandising BFA in Fashion Visual Merchandising Degrees Awarded in the Program(s) (2020): 29	Portfolio: Not req. Interview: Not req.
California State Polytechnic University, Pomona (CalPoly Pomona) 3801 West Temple Avenue, Pomona, CA 91768	GPA: N/A SAT (ERW): 500-610 SAT (M): 510-640 ACT (C): 19-27 ED: No	Admit Rate: 65% Undergrad Enrollment: 27,912 Total Enrollment: 30,014	BS in Apparel Merchandising and Management Degrees Awarded in the Program(s) (2020): 93	Portfolio: Not req. Interview: Not req.
California State University, Long Beach (CSULB) 1250 Bellflower Boulevard, Long Beach, CA 90840	GPA: 3.68 SAT (ERW): 510-620 SAT (M): 510-620 ACT (C): 20-26 ED: No	Admit Rate: 42% Undergrad Enrollment: 34,216 Total Enrollment: 40,069	BA in Family & Consumer Sciences, option: Fashion Merchandising Degrees Awarded in the Program(s) (2020): N/A	Portfolio: Not req. Interview: Not req.

School	Avg. GPA, SAT Evidence-Based Reading Writing (ERW), SAT Math (M), and ACT Composite (C) Early Decision (ED): Yes/No	Admission Statistics	Program(s)	Portfolio and/or Interview Required (Req.)
California State University, Northridge (CSUN) 18111 Nordhoff Street, Northridge, CA 91330	GPA: 3.39 SAT (ERW): 460-560 SAT (M): 440-550 ACT (C): 16-22 ED: No	Admit Rate: 66% Undergrad Enrollment: 34,916 Total Enrollment: 40,381	BS in Family and Consumer Sciences, concentration: Apparel Design and Merchandising Degrees Awarded in the Program(s) (2020): N/A	Portfolio: Not req. Interview: Not req.
Fashion Institute of Design and Merchandising (FIDM) 919 S. Grand Ave., Los Angeles, CA 90015	GPA: N/A SAT (ERW): N/A SAT (M): N/A ACT (C): N/A ED: No	Admit Rate: 39% Undergrad Enrollment: 1,847 Total Enrollment: 1,886	BS in Beauty Business Management Degrees Awarded in the Program(s) (2020): N/A	Portfolio: Req. Interview: Not req.
San Francisco State University 1600 Holloway Avenue - Burk Hall 329, San Francisco, CA 94132	GPA: 3.26 SAT (ERW): 470-580 SAT (M): 470-570 ACT (C): 17-23 ED: No	Admit Rate: 84% Undergrad Enrollment: 24,024 Total Enrollment: 27,349	BS in Apparel Design & Apparel Merchandising, concentration: Merchandising Degrees Awarded in the Program(s) (2020): 52	Portfolio: Not req. Interview: Not req.

WEST

FASHION MERCHANDISING PROGRAMS

School	Avg. GPA, SAT Evidence-Based Reading Writing (ERW), SAT Math (M), and ACT Composite (C) Early Decision (ED): Yes/No	Admission Statistics	Program(s)	Portfolio and/or Interview Required (Req.)
Colorado State University, Ft. Collins Colorado State University, Fort Collins, CO 80523	GPA: 3.7 SAT (ERW): 540-640 SAT (M): 530-640 ACT (C): 23-29 ED: No	Admit Rate: 84% Undergrad Enrollment: 24,792 Total Enrollment: 32,428	BS in Apparel and Merchandising, concentration: Merchandising Degrees Awarded in the Program(s) (2020): 78	Portfolio: Not req. Interview: Not req.
University of Hawaii at Manoa 2500 Campus Rd, Honolulu, HI 96822	GPA: 3.64 SAT (ERW): 540-630 SAT (M): 530-640 ACT (C): 21-26 ED: No	Admit Rate: 84% Undergrad Enrollment: 13,203 Total Enrollment: 18,025	BS in Fashion Design and Merchandising, specialization: Fashion Merchandising Degrees Awarded in the Program(s) (2020): 21	Portfolio: Not req. Interview: Not req.
Oregon State University Oregon State University, Corvallis, OR 97331	GPA: 3.62 SAT (ERW): 540-650 SAT (M): 540-660 ACT (C): 21-29 *Oregon State is test optional. ED: No	Admit Rate: 82% Undergrad Enrollment: 26,644 Total Enrollment: 32,312	BS in Merchandising Management Degrees Awarded in the Program(s) (2020): 50	Portfolio: Not req. Interview: Not req.
Washington State University Washington State University, Pullman, WA 99164	GPA: 3.46 SAT (ERW): 510-610 SAT (M): 510-600 ACT (C): 20-26 ED: No	Admit Rate: 80% Undergrad Enrollment: 25,470 Total Enrollment: 31,159	BA in Apparel, Merchandising, Design, and Textiles, option: Merchandising Degrees Awarded in the Program(s) (2020): 58	Portfolio: Not req. Interview: Not req.

ALASKA

ARIZONA

CALIFORNIA

COLORADO

HAWAII

IDAHO

MONTANA

NEVADA

NEW MEXICO

OREGON

UTAH

WASHINGTON

WYOMING

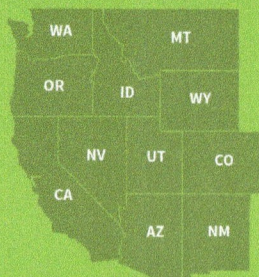

ACADEMY OF ART UNIVERSITY

Address: 79 New Montgomery St., San Francisco, CA 94105
Website: https://www.academyart.edu/academics/fashion/
Contact: https://my.academyart.edu/directories/admissions
Request for Information: https://www.academyart.edu/form-request-information/
Phone: (800) 544-2787
Email: admissions@academyart.edu

COST OF ATTENDANCE:

Tuition & Fees: $26,399 | **Additional Expenses:** N/A
Total: $26,399

Financial Aid: https://www.academyart.edu/finances/types-of-financial-aid/

ADDITIONAL INFORMATION:

Available Degree(s)

- BA in Fashion Journalism
- BFA in Fashion Marketing
- BFA in Fashion Merchandising
- BFA in Fashion Visual Merchandising

Freshman Portfolio Requirement

There is no portfolio. This is an open-admissions school.

Scholarships Offered

The Emerging Artist Scholarship offers awards up to $3,000. International Art & Design Scholarship awards a limited number of scholarships (up to $2,000) to international students. For more information, visit: https://www.academyart.edu/finances/scholarships/

Special Opportunities

Students may complete liberal arts requirements in Europe by taking a three-week intensive seminar. Every year, the School of Fashion awards two full-tuition scholarships for students who have passed the DELF B1 to study in Paris with Studio Berçot. Two students are selected to spend a year or a semester at the Fashion Department of Kingston University in London.

Notable Alumni

- Stephanie Thomas: Disability Fashion Jounrliast and Creator of Cur8able
- Ben Ellis: Co-Founder and Creative Director at ALIEN.ELEVEN
- Jacqueline Rabot: Co-Founder of Rabôt

CALIFORNIA STATE POLYTECHNIC UNIVERSITY, POMONA (CAL POLY POMONA)

Address: 3801 West Temple Avenue, Pomona, CA 91768
Website: https://www.cpp.edu/agri/apparel-merchandising-and-management/degree-requirements/about-this-major.shtml
Contact: https://www.cpp.edu/contact.shtml
Request for Information: https://www.cpp.edu/agri/applying/info-request.shtml
Phone: (909) 869-5299
Email: admissions@cpp.edu

COST OF ATTENDANCE:

In-State Tuition & Fees: $7,438 | **Additional Expenses:** $20,578
Total: $28,016

Out-of-State Tuition & Fees: $19,318 | **Additional Expenses:** $20,578
Total: $39,896

Financial Aid: https://www.cpp.edu/financial-aid/index.shtml

ADDITIONAL INFORMATION:

Available Degree(s)

- BS in Apparel Merchandising and Management

Freshman Portfolio Requirement

There is no portfolio requirement.

Scholarships Offered

Cal Poly Pomona has a Scholarship Fest application cycle that runs from October 1st through March 2nd. Students must apply via the Bronco Scholarship Portal. For more information, visit: https://www.cpp.edu/financial-aid/scholarships/cal-poly-pomona-scholarships.shtml

Special Opportunities

Students have the opportunity to produce a clothing line for the University Bookstore, study abroad in Italy, participate in an internship in the London fashion industry, and more.

Notable Alumni

- Teresa Becker: Designer and Owner at Heart of Haute
- Sarah Dumlao: Global Supply Planner at Nike

ALASKA

ARIZONA

CALIFORNIA

COLORADO

HAWAII

IDAHO

MONTANA

NEVADA

NEW MEXICO

OREGON

UTAH

WASHINGTON

WYOMING

WEST

ALASKA

ARIZONA

CALIFORNIA

COLORADO

HAWAII

IDAHO

MONTANA

NEVADA

NEW MEXICO

OREGON

UTAH

WASHINGTON

WYOMING

CALIFORNIA STATE UNIVERSITY, LONG BEACH

Address: 1250 Bellflower Boulevard, Long Beach, CA 90840
Website: https://www.csulb.edu/college-of-health-human-services/family-and-consumer-sciences/fashion-merchandising
Contact: https://www.csulb.edu/contact
Request for Information: https://web.csulb.edu/divisions/students/uosr/request_info.html
Phone: (562) 985-4111
Email: eslb@csulb.edu

COST OF ATTENDANCE:

In-State Tuition & Fees: $6,846 | **Additional Expenses:** $18,206
Total: $25,386

Out-of-State Tuition & Fees: $17,142 | **Additional Expenses:** $18,540
Total: $35,682

Financial Aid: https://www.csulb.edu/student-affairs/financial-aid-and-scholarships-office

ADDITIONAL INFORMATION:

Available Degree(s)

- BA in Family & Consumer Sciences, option: Fashion Merchandising

Freshman Portfolio Requirement

There is no portfolio requirement.

Scholarships Offered

The President's Scholars Program offers merit-based scholarships to students admitted to the University Honors Program (UHP). Students may apply for BeachScholarships once they are admitted into CSULB. For more information, visit: https://www.csulb.edu/student-affairs/financial-aid-and-scholarships-office/prospective-students

Special Opportunities

Fashion students may participate in a fashion study tour where they visit museums, apparel manufacturers, retailers, and apparel design businesses. Tours are conducted throughout the year in locations such as New York City, Paris, and Italy.

Notable Alumni

- Dezarae Jackson: Site Merchandiser at REVOLVE
- Zggoe (Zee-Go) Kayasitt: Assistant Stylist at Styling Life Inc.

CALIFORNIA STATE UNIVERSITY, NORTHRIDGE (CSUN)

Address: 18111 Nordhoff Street, Northridge, CA 91330
Website: https://www.csun.edu/health-human-development/
family-consumer-sciences/program-overview-0
Contact: https://www.csun.edu/contact
Request for Information: N/A
Phone: (818) 677-1200
Email: outreach.recruitment.@csun.edu

COST OF ATTENDANCE:

In-State Tuition & Fees: $6,972 | **Additional Expenses:** $16,670
Total: $23,642

Out-of-State Tuition & Fees: $16,476 | **Additional Expenses:** $16,670
Total: $33,146

Financial Aid: https://www.csun.edu/financialaid/financial-aid-basics

ADDITIONAL INFORMATION:

Available Degree(s)

- BS in Family and Consumer Sciences, concentration: Apparel Design and Merchandising

Freshman Portfolio Requirement

There is no portfolio requirement.

Scholarships Offered

CSUN offers several different scholarships to incoming students. It is suggested that students look through current scholarship opportunities, as they are constantly changing. For more information, visit: https://csun.academicworks.com/

Special Opportunities

CSUN houses a collection of historical garments that are displayed in galleries on campus as a visual aid for students during lectures.

Notable Alumni

- Alexus Green: Former Lead of Merchandising at Fashion Nova
- Maria Juarez: Sample Coordinator at Fashion Nova

ALASKA

ARIZONA

CALIFORNIA

COLORADO

HAWAII

IDAHO

MONTANA

NEVADA

NEW MEXICO

OREGON

UTAH

WASHINGTON

WYOMING

WEST

ALASKA

ARIZONA

CALIFORNIA

COLORADO

HAWAII

IDAHO

MONTANA

NEVADA

NEW MEXICO

OREGON

UTAH

WASHINGTON

WYOMING

FASHION INSTITUTE OF DESIGN AND MERCHANDISING (FIDM)

Address: 919 S. Grand Ave., Los Angeles, CA 90015
Website: https://fidm.edu/en/majors/
beauty+business+management/
Contact: https://fidm.edu/en/about/contact+us/
Request for Information: https://go.fidm.edu/info
Phone: (800) 624-1200
Email: admissions@fidm.edu
Other locations: San Francisco, CA; Irvine, CA; San Diego, CA

COST OF ATTENDANCE:

Tuition & Fees: $31,465 | **Additional Expenses:** $22,373
Total: $53,838

Financial Aid: https://fidm.edu/en/admissions/financial+aid/

ADDITIONAL INFORMATION:

Available Degree(s)

- BS in Beauty Business Management

Freshman Portfolio Requirement
To enter the BS in Beauty Business Management or any baccalaureate program, applicants must complete an AA degree first. Related AA degrees to consider include: Merchandise Product Development ; Merchandising & Marketing; and Beauty Marketing & Product Development.

Note: AA Advanced Study degrees are also offered. However, these degrees are for students who already hold a degree.

- Response to the following prompt with an essay (minimum 2 pages) OR a link to your work in another medium, for example, a two-minute video.

Prompt: Select an existing product, brand, or design that shows innovation in form, function, and purpose or is a benefit to culture/society. What is the cultural relevance of your concept in today's society and how does it compare to similar products, brands, or designs that already exist? Tell or show us what makes this work great in your own opinion.

For more information, visit: https://fidm.edu/en/admissions/how+to+apply/

Scholarships Offered
The FCCLA National Scholarship Competition offers a full year of tuition to first place winners. In addition, high school juniors who are active members of the official FIDM Fashion Club are eligible to enter the FIDM Fashion Club Junior Scholarship Competition. High school seniors may be eligible for the FIDM National Scholarship Competition (covering one year of tuition). For more information, visit: https://fidm.edu/en/admissions/financial+aid/scholarships/

Special Opportunities
Students are encouraged to embark on one of the Study Tours – domestic and international opportunities for students. Study tours consist of an expert guiding the tour and many of these experiences include a networking element. Study tours take place in France, Italy, and China. For more information, visit: https://fidm.edu/en/student+life/study+abroad/study+tours/

SAN FRANCISCO STATE UNIVERSITY

Address: 1600 Holloway Avenue - Burk Hall 329, San Francisco, CA 94132
Website: https://fina.sfsu.edu/adm
Contact: https://fina.sfsu.edu/contactus
Request for Information: N/A
Phone: (415) 338-1219
Email: fina@sfsu.edu

COST OF ATTENDANCE:

In-State Tuition & Fees: $7,270 | **Additional Expenses:** $18,858
Total: $26,128

Out-of-State Tuition & Fees: $16,774 | **Additional Expenses:** $18,858
Total: $35,632

Financial Aid: https://financialaid.sfsu.edu/

ADDITIONAL INFORMATION:

Available Degree(s)

- BS in Apparel Design & Apparel Merchandising, concentration: Merchandising

Freshman Portfolio Requirement

There is no portfolio requirement.

Scholarships Offered

The Department of Family, Interiors, Nutrition, and Apparel (FINA) offers scholarships specific to FINA students. Students are encouraged to visit the link for more information, since scholarship availability changes throughout the course of the year. For more information, visit: https://fina.sfsu.edu/content/student-resources#Scholarships

Special Opportunities

Students are encouraged to study abroad. For more information, visit: https://oip.sfsu.edu/sfstateabroad

ALASKA

ARIZONA

CALIFORNIA

COLORADO

HAWAII

IDAHO

MONTANA

NEVADA

NEW MEXICO

OREGON

UTAH

WASHINGTON

WYOMING

WEST

ALASKA

ARIZONA

CALIFORNIA

COLORADO

HAWAII

IDAHO

MONTANA

NEVADA

NEW MEXICO

OREGON

UTAH

WASHINGTON

WYOMING

COLORADO STATE UNIVERSITY, FT. COLLINS

Address: Colorado State University, Fort Collins, CO 80523
Website: https://www.chhs.colostate.edu/dm/programs-and-degrees/b-s-in-apparel-and-merchandising/merchandising-concentration/
Contact: https://admissions.colostate.edu/contactus/
Request for Information: https://www.chhs.colostate.edu/academics/request-info/
Phone: (970) 491-6331
Email: chhsinfo@colostate.edu

COST OF ATTENDANCE:

In-State Tuition & Fees: $12,432 | **Additional Expenses:** $17,163
Total: $29,595

Out-of-State Tuition & Fees: $31,712 | **Additional Expenses:** $17,862
Total: $49,574

Financial Aid: https://financialaid.colostate.edu/

ADDITIONAL INFORMATION:

Available Degree(s)

- BS in Apparel and Merchandising, concentration: Merchandising

Freshman Portfolio Requirement

There is no portfolio requirement.

Scholarships Offered

The College of Health and Human Sciences offers a few scholarship opportunities to students within this department. Fashion students may be eligible for the Students First Scholarship, which awards students who are active in community service organizations and have a 3.0+ GPA. For more information on available College of Health and Human Sciences scholarships, visit: https://www.chhs.colostate.edu/academics/scholarships/

Special Opportunities

Every other year, the Department offers a study tour of New York City to students. This week-long trip has "students [visiting] firms in the apparel and interior design industries and engage in a variety of cultural and entertainment activities, which may include visiting historic sites and museums, taking in a Manhattan dinner cruise, and attending Broadway shows."

International study tours are also available and highly relevant to Apparel & Merchandising students. Previous destinations have been in Hong Kong, Thailand, and England/Scotland. For more information, visit: https://www.chhs.colostate.edu/dm/programs-and-degrees/advising-and-support/study-tours-and-education-abroad/

UNIVERSITY OF HAWAII AT MANOA

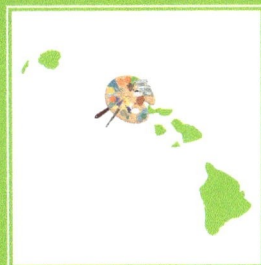

Address: 2500 Campus Rd, Honolulu, HI 96822
Website: https://cms.ctahr.hawaii.edu/Majors/FDM
Contact: https://manoa.hawaii.edu/about/contact/
Request for Information: https://manoa.hawaii.edu/admissions/request/
Phone: (800) 823-9771
Email: uhmanoa.admissions@hawaii.edu

COST OF ATTENDANCE:

In-State Tuition & Fees: $12,186 | **Additional Expenses:** $17,734
Total: $29,920

WUE* Tuition & Fees: $17,838 | **Additional Expenses:** $17,734
Total: $35,572

Out-of-State Tuition & Fees: $34,218 | **Additional Expenses:** $17,734
Total: $51,952

*Western Undergraduate Exchange (WUE) is a special tuition program for students from certain states. For a list of eligible states, visit: https://manoa.hawaii.edu/admissions/financing/wue.html

Financial Aid: https://manoa.hawaii.edu/admissions/financing/index.html

ADDITIONAL INFORMATION:

Available Degree(s)

- BS in Fashion Design and Merchandising, specialization: Fashion Merchandising

Freshman Portfolio Requirement

There is no portfolio requirement.

Scholarships Offered

The College of Tropical Agriculture and Human Resources (CTAHR) offers incoming fashion students scholarship opportunities that range from $2,000 upwards. For more information, visit: https://cms.ctahr.hawaii.edu/Students/Scholarships

There are also a few scholarships for fashion students while they are undergraduates. For more information, visit: https://cms.ctahr.hawaii.edu/fcs/Undergraduate/FDM/Scholarships

Additionally, incoming in-state, out-of-state, and international students may be eligible for merit-based scholarships. For more information, visit: http://www.hawaii.edu/fas/info/automatic_admissions_scholarships.php

Special Opportunities

UHM hosts an annual fashion show where apparel design students showcase their work. For more information, visit: https://cms.ctahr.hawaii.edu/fcs2/Undergraduate/FDM/UHM-Fashion-Shows

ALASKA

ARIZONA

CALIFORNIA

COLORADO

HAWAII

IDAHO

MONTANA

NEVADA

NEW MEXICO

OREGON

UTAH

WASHINGTON

WYOMING

WEST

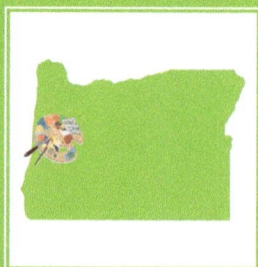

ALASKA

ARIZONA

CALIFORNIA

COLORADO

HAWAII

IDAHO

MONTANA

NEVADA

NEW MEXICO

OREGON

UTAH

WASHINGTON

WYOMING

OREGON STATE UNIVERSITY

Address: Oregon State University, Corvallis, OR 97331
Website: https://business.oregonstate.edu/programs/
undergraduate/merchandising-management
Contact: https://admissions.oregonstate.edu/contact-information
Request for Information: https://admissions.oregonstate.edu/
send-me-info
Phone: (541) 737-4411
Email: osuadmit@oregonstate.edu

COST OF ATTENDANCE:

In-State Tuition & Fees: $12,165 | **Additional Expenses:** $17,142
Total: $29,307

Out-of-State Tuition & Fees: $32,355 | **Additional Expenses:** $17,142
Total: $49,497

Financial Aid: https://financialaid.oregonstate.edu/

ADDITIONAL INFORMATION:

Available Degree(s)

- BS in Merchandising Management

Freshman Portfolio Requirement

There is no portfolio requirement.

Scholarships Offered

Oregon State offers institutional aid to students of any major.
Out-of-state applicants may be eligible for the Provost Scholarship,
or specific scholarships only available to CA, WA, HI, or ID
residents. Oregon State residents may be eligible for the merit-
based Presidential Scholarship (up to $10,000 per year for four
years), or a number of other scholarships. For more information,
visit: https://scholarships.oregonstate.edu/prospective-student-
scholarships

Special Opportunities

Students may study abroad at the Accademia Italiana in Florence,
Italy, the London College of Fashion, or Hanyang University in
Seoul. For more information, visit: http://business.oregonstate.edu/
student-experience/student-success/study-abroad

Notable Alumni

- Evietta Chapman: Merchandise Coordinator at Men's
  Sportswear
- Kristy Milien: Merchandise Business Office Assistant at Macy's

WASHINGTON STATE UNIVERSITY

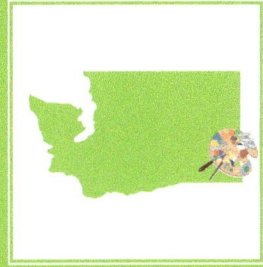

Address: Washington State University, Pullman, WA 99164
Website: http://amdt.wsu.edu/major/
Contact: https://admission.wsu.edu/contact/
Request for Information: https://admission.wsu.edu/contact/
request-info/
Phone: (888) 468-6978
Email: admissions@wsu.edu

COST OF ATTENDANCE:

In-State Tuition & Fees: $12,416 | **Additional Expenses:** $12,082
Total: $24,498

Out-of-State Tuition & Fees: $27,732 | **Additional Expenses:** $12,082
Total: $39,814

Financial Aid: https://admission.wsu.edu/tuition-costs/tuition-
break-down/

ADDITIONAL INFORMATION:

Available Degree(s)

- BA in Apparel, Merchandising, Design, and Textiles, option:
  Merchandising

Freshman Portfolio Requirement

There is no portfolio requirement.

Scholarships Offered

The College of Agricultural, Human, and Natural Resource Sciences
offer departmental scholarships the range in value from $100 to
$4,000. Apparel, Merchandising, Design, & Textile (AMDT) students
are eligible for these. Students can gain access to these awards
by applying to the WSU online scholarship application. For more
information, visit: https://cahnrs.wsu.edu/academics/scholarships/?

There are many scholarships specific to Washington residents, out-
of-state students, and international students. In-state scholarships
are merit and/or need-based and go up to full tuition. Out-of-state
scholarships go up to $11,000 per year, for four years. International
scholarships range from $1,000-$2,000 per semester. For more
information, visit: https://admission.wsu.edu/scholarships/

Special Opportunities

Given the global nature of the fashion world, AMDT students are
especially encouraged to study abroad. WSU suggests that students
plan early in their college career due to sequencing of courses. In
addition, summers abroad are the most preferable choice for AMDT
majors.

ALASKA

ARIZONA

CALIFORNIA

COLORADO

HAWAII

IDAHO

MONTANA

NEVADA

NEW MEXICO

OREGON

UTAH

WASHINGTON

WYOMING

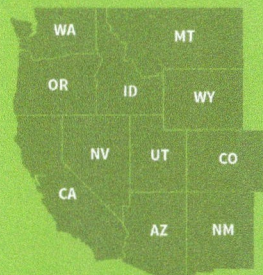

WEST

CHAPTER 15

FASHION MERCHANDISING SCHOOLS ALPHABETIZED BY CITY/STATE

Fashion School	City	State
Auburn University	Auburn	Alabama
California State University, Long Beach (CSULB)	Long Beach	California
Fashion Institute of Design and Merchandising (FIDM)	Los Angeles	California
California State University, Northridge (CSUN)	Northridge	California
California State Polytechnic University, Pomona (CalPoly Pomona)	Pomona	California
Academy of Art University	San Francisco	California
San Francisco State University	San Francisco	California
Colorado State University, Ft. Collins	Fort Collins	Colorado
University of Delaware	Newark	Delaware
Miami International University Art & Design	Miami	Florida
Florida State University	Tallahassee	Florida
University of Georgia	Athens	Georgia
Savannah College of Art & Design (SCAD)	Savannah	Georgia
University of Hawaii at Manoa	Honolulu	Hawaii
Columbia College Chicago	Chicago	Illinois
Dominican University	River Forest	Illinois
Indiana University at Bloomington	Bloomington	Indiana
Iowa State University	Ames	Iowa
Kansas State University	Manhattan	Kansas
Louisiana State University	Baton Rouge	Louisiana
University of Minnesota	Minneapolis	Minnesota
Stephens College	Columbia	Missouri
University of Missouri	Columbia	Missouri
University of Nebraska	Lincoln	Nebraska
Cornell University	Ithaca	New York
Fashion Institute of Technology (FIT)	New York	New York
LIM College	New York	New York

Fashion School	City	State
Parsons - The New School	New York	New York
Marist College	Poughkeepsie	New York
University of North Carolina, Greensboro	Greensboro	North Carolina
North Carolina State University, Raleigh College of Design	Raleigh	North Carolina
The Ohio State University	Columbus	Ohio
Kent State University	Kent	Ohio
Oklahoma State University	Stillwater	Oklahoma
Oregon State University	Corvallis	Oregon
Drexel University	Philadelphia	Pennsylvania
Thomas Jefferson University	Philadelphia	Pennsylvania
University of Rhode Island	South Kingston	Rhode Island
University of South Carolina	Columbia	South Carolina
University of Texas, Austin (UT Austin)	Austin	Texas
Southern Methodist University (SMU)	Dallas	Texas
Texas Woman's University	Denton	Texas
University of North Texas	Denton	Texas
Texas Tech University	Lubbock	Texas
University of the Incarnate Word	San Antonio	Texas
Baylor University	Waco	Texas
Virginia Tech University	Blacksburg	Virginia
Virginia Commonwealth University	Richmond	Virginia
Washington State University	Pullman	Washington
West Virginia University	Morgantown	West Virginia

CHAPTER 16

TOP 10 FASHION MERCHANDISING SCHOOLS

Ranking	School
1	Fashion Institute of Technology (FIT)
2	Fashion Institute of Design & Merchandising (FIDM)
3	Savannah College of Art & Design (SCAD)
4	Drexel University
5	Parsons - The New School
6	Cornell University
7	North Carolina State University
8	Iowa State University
9	LIM College
10	Kent State University

CHAPTER 17

FASHION MERCHANDISING SCHOOLS BY AVERAGE TEST SCORE

FASHION MERCHANDISING SCHOOLS BY AVERAGE SAT SCORE

Fashion School	Avg. SAT
California State University, Northridge (CSUN)	460-560 (ERW) 440-550 (M)
San Francisco State University	470-580 (ERW) 470-570 (M)
Texas Woman's University	480-580 (ERW) 460-560 (M)
University of the Incarnate Word	480-580 (ERW) 470-560 (M)
Dominican University	480-580 (ERW) 480-580 (M)
Iowa State University	480-630 (ERW) 530-680 (M)
University of North Carolina, Greensboro	490-590 (ERW) 490-570 (M)
California State Polytechnic University, Pomona (CalPoly Pomona)	500-610 (ERW) 510-640 (M)
Kent State University	510-610 (ERW) 510-600 (M)
Washington State University	510-610 (ERW) 510-600 (M)
California State University, Long Beach (CSULB)	510-620 (ERW) 510-620 (M)
West Virginia University	520-620 (ERW) 510-610 (M)
University of North Texas	530-630 (ERW) 520-610 (M)
Texas Tech University	540-620 (ERW) 530-620 (M)
University of Hawaii at Manoa	540-630 (ERW) 530-640 (M)
Savannah College of Art & Design (SCAD)	540-640 (ERW) 500-600 (M)
Virginia Commonwealth University	540-640 (ERW) 520-610 (M)

Fashion School	Avg. SAT
Oklahoma State University	540-640 (ERW)
	520-640 (M)
Colorado State University, Ft. Collins	540-640 (ERW)
	530-640 (M)
Oregon State University	540-650 (ERW)
	540-660 (M)
University of Rhode Island	550-630 (ERW)
	540-630 (M)
Thomas Jefferson University	550-630 (ERW)
	540-640 (M)
University of Nebraska	550-650 (ERW)
	560-670 (M)
Louisiana State University	550-660 (ERW)
	540-640 (M)
University of Missouri	560-660 (ERW)
	550-660 (M)
Indiana University at Bloomington	560-670 (ERW)
	560-680 (M)
Marist College	580-660 (ERW)
	560-660 (M)
University of Delaware	580-660 (ERW)
	570-670 (M)
University of South Carolina	580-670 (ERW)
	560-670 (M)
Parsons - The New School	580-680 (ERW)
	560-680 (M)
Auburn University	590-650 (ERW)
	570-670 (M)
Virginia Tech University	590-680 (ERW)
	580-690 (M)
Drexel University	590-680 (ERW)
	590-700 (M)
The Ohio State University	590-690 (ERW)
	620-740 (M)

Fashion School	Avg. SAT
Baylor University	600-680 (ERW)
	590-680 (M)
Stephens College	600-700 (ERW)
	640-760 (M)
University of Minnesota	600-700 (ERW)
	640-760 (M)
University of Texas, Austin (UT Austin)	610-720 (ERW)
	600-750 (M)
Florida State University	620-680 (ERW)
	600-670 (M)
North Carolina State University, Raleigh College of Design	620-690 (ERW)
	630-730 (M)
University of Georgia	620-700 (ERW)
	600-720 (M)
Southern Methodist University (SMU)	640-720 (ERW)
	660-760 (M)
Cornell University	680-750 (ERW)
	720-790 (M)
Kansas State University	N/A
Academy of Art University	N/A *Open admissions
Miami International University Art & Design	N/A *Open admissions
Columbia College Chicago	N/A
	*Test optional
Fashion Institute of Technology (FIT)	N/A
	*Test optional
LIM College	N/A
	*Test optional
Fashion Institute of Design and Merchandising (FIDM)	N/A *Test optional

FASHION MERCHANDISING SCHOOLS BY AVERAGE ACT SCORE

Fashion School	Avg. ACT
California State University, Northridge (CSUN)	16-22 (ACT C)
Texas Woman's University	16-22 (ACT C)
San Francisco State University	17-23 (ACT C)
University of the Incarnate Word	17-23 (ACT C)
Dominican University	19-24 (ACT C)
University of North Carolina, Greensboro	19-25 (ACT C)
California State Polytechnic University, Pomona (CalPoly Pomona)	19-27 (ACT C)
California State University, Long Beach (CSULB)	20-26 (ACT C)
Kent State University	20-26 (ACT C)
Washington State University	20-26 (ACT C)
Kansas State University	20-27 (ACT C)
Savannah College of Art & Design (SCAD)	20-27 (ACT C)
Thomas Jefferson University	20-27 (ACT C)
University of North Texas	20-27 (ACT C)
University of Hawaii at Manoa	21-26 (ACT C)
West Virginia University	21-27 (ACT C)
Iowa State University	21-28 (ACT C)
Virginia Commonwealth University	21-28 (ACT C)
Oregon State University	21-29 (ACT C)
Texas Tech University	22-27 (ACT C)
Oklahoma State University	22-28 (ACT C)
University of Nebraska	22-28 (ACT C)
Louisiana State University	23-28 (ACT C)
University of Rhode Island	23-28 (ACT C)
Colorado State University, Ft. Collins	23-29 (ACT C)
University of Missouri	23-29 (ACT C)
Indiana University at Bloomington	24-31 (ACT C)
University of Delaware	25-30 (ACT C)
Auburn University	25-31 (ACT C)
Drexel University	25-31 (ACT C)
Stephens College	25-31 (ACT C)
University of Minnesota	25-31 (ACT C)
University of South Carolina	25-31 (ACT C)
Virginia Tech University	25-31 (ACT C)
Parsons - The New School	26-30 (ACT C)

Fashion School	Avg. ACT
Baylor University	26-31 (ACT C)
Marist College	26-31 (ACT C)
The Ohio State University	26-32 (ACT C)
University of Texas, Austin (UT Austin)	26-33 (ACT C)
Florida State University	27-31 (ACT C)
North Carolina State University, Raleigh College of Design	27-32 (ACT C)
University of Georgia	27-32 (ACT C)
Southern Methodist University (SMU)	29-33 (ACT C)
Cornell University	32-35 (ACT C)
Academy of Art University	N/A *Open admissions
Miami International University Art & Design	N/A *Open admissions
Columbia College Chicago	N/A *Test optional
Fashion Institute of Technology (FIT)	N/A *Test optional
LIM College	N/A *Test optional
Fashion Institute of Design and Merchandising (FIDM)	N/A *Test optional

FASHION MERCHANDISING SCHOOLS BY AVERAGE GPA

Fashion School	Avg. GPA
Texas Woman's University	3.17
San Francisco State University	3.26
California State University, Northridge (CSUN)	3.39
Marist College	3.4
Louisiana State University	3.45
Washington State University	3.46
University of South Carolina	3.53
University of Rhode Island	3.56
University of the Incarnate Word	3.56
Oklahoma State University	3.59
Savannah College of Art & Design (SCAD)	3.6
University of Nebraska	3.6
Kent State University	3.61
Kansas State University	3.62
Oregon State University	3.62
Texas Tech University	3.63
Southern Methodist University (SMU)	3.64
University of Hawaii at Manoa	3.64
University of North Carolina, Greensboro	3.67
California State University, Long Beach (CSULB)	3.68
Colorado State University, Ft. Collins	3.7
Iowa State University	3.71
Dominican University	3.72
Virginia Commonwealth University	3.72
Indiana University at Bloomington	3.75
North Carolina State University, Raleigh College of Design	3.8
University of Delaware	3.92
Virginia Tech University	3.96
Auburn University	3.97
University of Georgia	4.02
Florida State University	4.16
Baylor University	N/A
Columbia College Chicago	N/A
Cornell University	N/A
Drexel University	N/A

Fashion School	Avg. GPA
Fashion Institute of Design and Merchandising (FIDM)	N/A
Fashion Institute of Technology (FIT)	N/A
LIM College	N/A
Parsons - The New School	N/A
Stephens College	N/A
The Ohio State University	N/A
Thomas Jefferson University	N/A
University of Minnesota	N/A
University of Missouri	N/A
University of North Texas	N/A
University of Texas, Austin (UT Austin)	N/A
West Virginia University	N/A
California State Polytechnic University, Pomona (CalPoly Pomona)	N/A
Academy of Art University	N/A *Open admissions
Miami International University Art & Design	N/A *Open admissions

JOURNEY TO ART, DANCE, MUSIC, THEATRE, FILM, AND FASHION SERIES

JOURNEY TO
Fashion Design
COLLEGE ADMISSIONS & PROFILES

RACHEL A. WINSTON, PH.D.

JOURNEY TO
Fashion Merchandising
COLLEGE ADMISSIONS & PROFILES

RACHEL A. WINSTON, PH.D.

JOURNEY TO
Costume Design & Technical Theatre
COLLEGE ADMISSIONS & PROFILES

RACHEL A. WINSTON, PH.D.

JOURNEY TO
Theatre and the Dramatic Arts
COLLEGE ADMISSIONS & PROFILES

RACHEL A. WINSTON, PH.D.

JOURNEY TO
Musical
Theatre
COLLEGE ADMISSIONS & PROFILES

RACHEL A. WINSTON, PH.D.

***Live your dreams today remembering that discipline is the
bridge between dreams and achievement!***

"We believe in the American Dream that all people rich or poor can
go as far in life as their talents and persistence will take them."
– Lizard Publishing Vision

At Lizard, we help you make your dreams come true.

CONTACT INFORMATION

Phone: 949-833-7706
E-mail: collegeguide@yahoo.com
Website: collegelizard.com and Lizard-publishing.com

COMPREHENSIVE HEALTH CARE SERIES

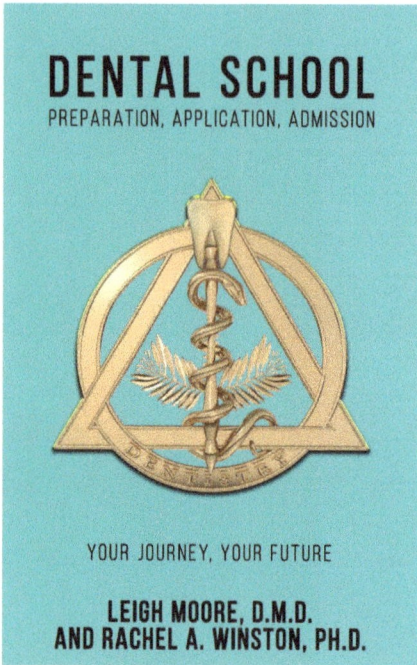

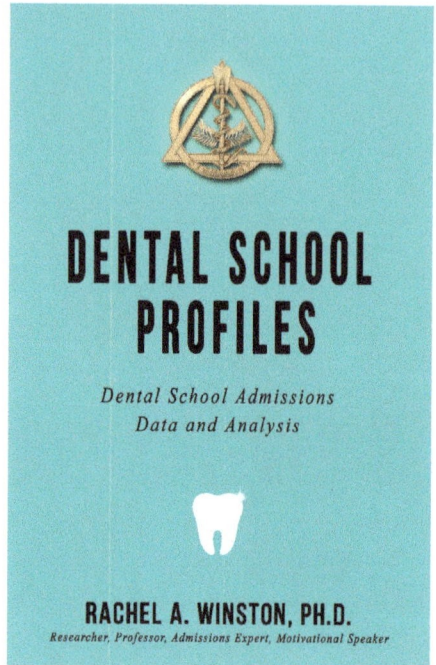

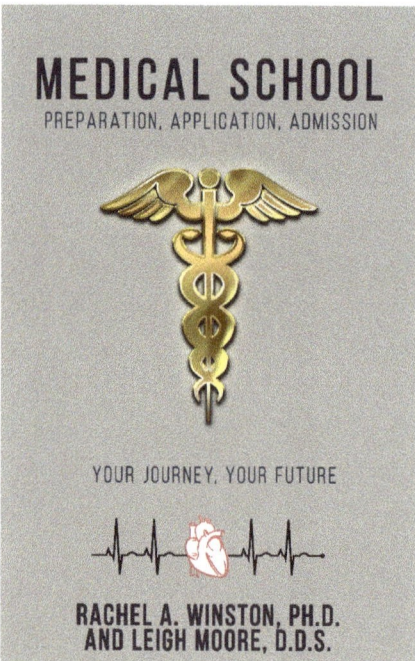

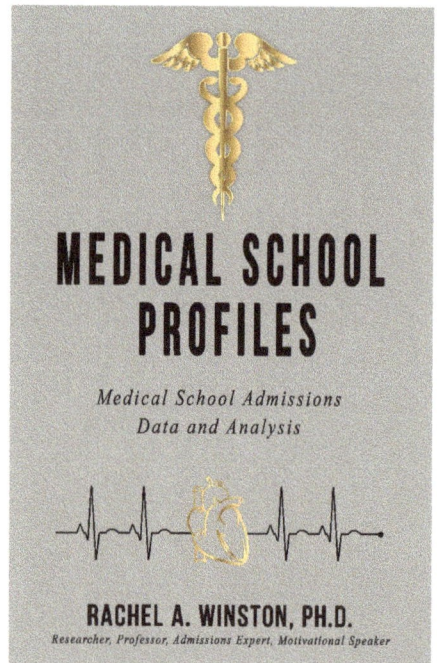

DENTAL SCHOOL
PREPARATION, APPLICATION, ADMISSION

YOUR JOURNEY, YOUR FUTURE

**LEIGH MOORE, D.M.D.
AND RACHEL A. WINSTON, PH.D.**

DENTAL SCHOOL PROFILES

*Dental School Admissions
Data and Analysis*

RACHEL A. WINSTON, PH.D.
Researcher, Professor, Admissions Expert, Motivational Speaker

MEDICAL SCHOOL
PREPARATION, APPLICATION, ADMISSION

YOUR JOURNEY, YOUR FUTURE

**RACHEL A. WINSTON, PH.D.
AND LEIGH MOORE, D.D.S.**

MEDICAL SCHOOL PROFILES

*Medical School Admissions
Data and Analysis*

RACHEL A. WINSTON, PH.D.
Researcher, Professor, Admissions Expert, Motivational Speaker

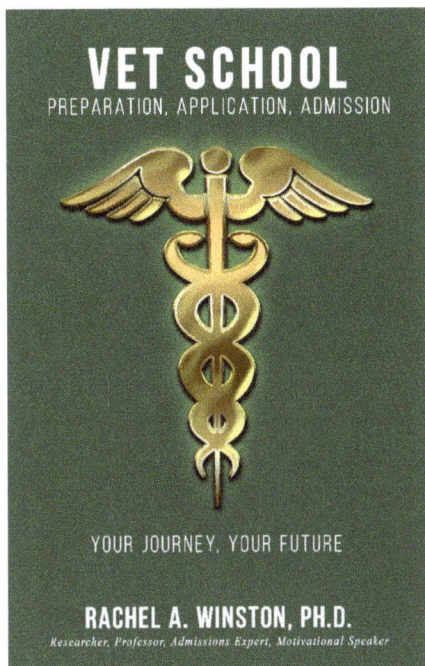
VET SCHOOL
PREPARATION, APPLICATION, ADMISSION

YOUR JOURNEY, YOUR FUTURE

RACHEL A. WINSTON, PH.D.
Researcher, Professor, Admissions Expert, Motivational Speaker

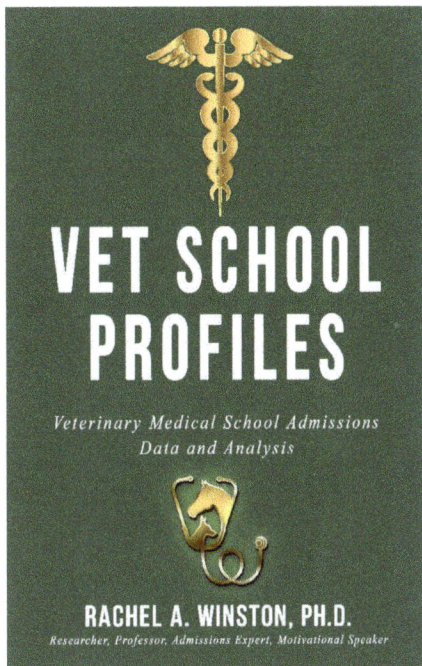
VET SCHOOL PROFILES

Veterinary Medical School Admissions Data and Analysis

RACHEL A. WINSTON, PH.D.
Researcher, Professor, Admissions Expert, Motivational Speaker

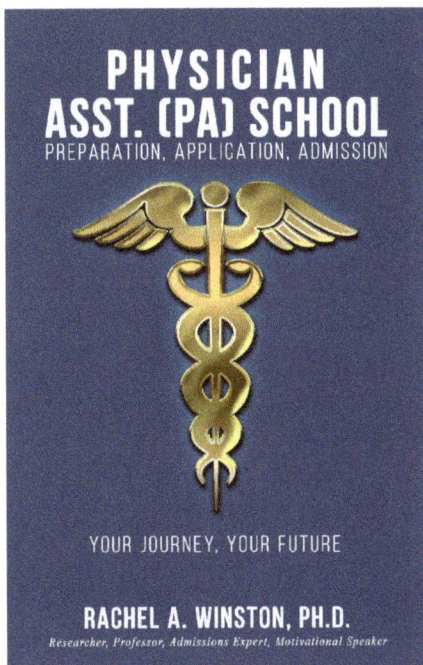
PHYSICIAN ASST. (PA) SCHOOL
PREPARATION, APPLICATION, ADMISSION

YOUR JOURNEY, YOUR FUTURE

RACHEL A. WINSTON, PH.D.
Researcher, Professor, Admissions Expert, Motivational Speaker

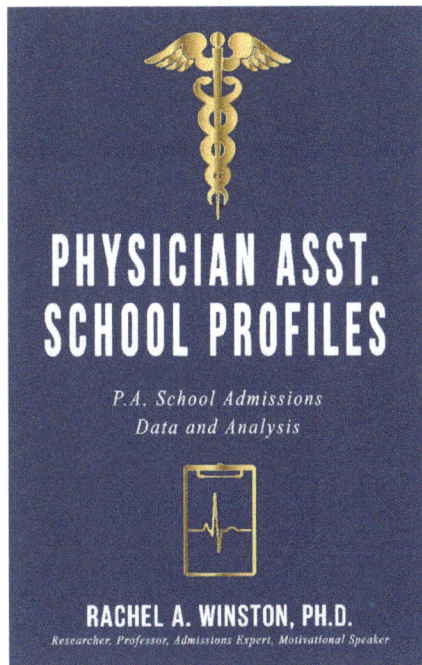
PHYSICIAN ASST. SCHOOL PROFILES

P.A. School Admissions Data and Analysis

RACHEL A. WINSTON, PH.D.
Researcher, Professor, Admissions Expert, Motivational Speaker

PHARM.D. SCHOOL
PREPARATION, APPLICATION, ADMISSION

YOUR JOURNEY, YOUR FUTURE

RACHEL A. WINSTON, PH.D.
Researcher, Professor, Admissions Expert, Motivational Speaker

PHARM.D. SCHOOL PROFILES

Pharmacy School Admissions Data and Analysis

RACHEL A. WINSTON, PH.D.
Researcher, Professor, Admissions Expert, Motivational Speaker

OSTEOPATHIC MEDICAL SCHOOL
PREPARATION, APPLICATION, ADMISSION

YOUR JOURNEY, YOUR FUTURE

RACHEL A. WINSTON, PH.D.
Researcher, Professor, Admissions Expert, Motivational Speaker

OSTEO SCHOOL PROFILES

Osteopathic Medical School Admissions Data and Analysis

RACHEL A. WINSTON, PH.D.
Researcher, Professor, Admissions Expert, Motivational Speaker

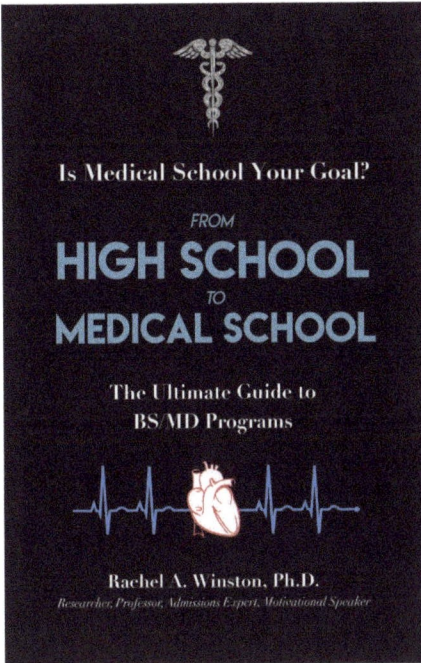

This comprehensive healthcare series is designed in full color to aid the growing number of applicants seeking clear, comprehensive materials. As a college admissions expert and former UCLA College Counseling Certificate Program faculty member, Dr. Winston is dedicated to helping students obtain the information they need.

FOR MORE INFORMATION

bsmdguide.com

medschoolexpert.com

Purchase books at Lizard-publishing.com

Is Medical School Your Goal?

FROM

HIGH SCHOOL
TO
MEDICAL SCHOOL

The Ultimate Guide to
BS/MD Programs

Rachel A. Winston, Ph.D.
Researcher, Professor, Admissions Expert, Motivational Speaker

SERVICES OFFERED BY LIZARD EDUCATION:

- College Counseling
- Admissions News/Resources
- Essay Support and Editing
- Interview Preparation
- Road Trips to Visit Colleges
- Career Planning/Majors/ Resumes
- BS/MD, BS/DO, BS/JD, BS/DDS
- Medical School
- Graduate School (Masters & Doctorate)
- Film Studio and Editing
- Portfolio Assistance/SlideRoom
- Athletics Recruiting/Highlight Films
- International Admissions/Visa/ TOEFL
- Financial Aid and Scholarships
- UCs, Ivy Leagues, and Colleges Nationwide
- Book Publishing
- Engineering, Robotics, STEM
- Art Portfolios

Email: collegeguide@yahoo.com

Website: collegelizard.com

LIZARD

INDEX

A

ACT 66, 68, 69, 92, 93, 94, 106, 107, 108, 109, 113, 119, 124, 125, 126, 127, 128, 129, 130, 131, 141, 152, 156, 157, 158, 180, 181

Admissions i, viii, 63, 66, 102, 144, 189

Advertising viii, 27, 64, 97

Apparel 5, 58, 66, 79, 94, 96, 103, 106, 107, 108, 112, 113, 117, 118, 124, 126, 127, 130, 131, 132, 133, 134, 135, 138, 140, 143, 145, 148, 151, 152, 156, 157, 158, 161, 163, 165, 166, 169

Audition 66, 110

B

Bachelor's Degree 52, 77

BFA viii, 45, 46, 47, 48, 49, 50, 51, 52, 53, 64, 66, 92, 108, 116, 125, 136, 156, 160

Bureau of Labor Statistics 77

C

Casualization 31

Chapter 11 ix, 30

CLEP 51

Coalition Application 70

Common App 70

Common Application 70

Consumer 14, 18, 76, 78, 118, 126, 130, 132, 137, 140, 143, 148, 156, 157, 162, 163

Coresight Research 9

Costume Designer 58, 78

CSS Profile 73

Cybercrime 60, 61

D

Defer 73

DropBox 40

E

Early Action 69

Early Decision 69, 70, 92, 93, 106, 107, 124, 125, 156, 157

E-commerce vii, 3, 5, 8, 23, 30, 76

Employment viii, 75

Essays vi, vii, 68, 70

Extortion 60

F

Fabric 64, 79

FAFSA 73, 100

Financial Aid 52, 57, 72, 73, 96

Footwear 58, 64

Forecast 8, 13

Forgery 60

G

Graphic design viii, 13, 27, 28, 48, 50, 78

I

IB 47, 51, 68, 69

Intellectual Property 60

Internships 34, 36, 38, 41, 42, 48, 51, 52, 56, 66, 77, 114

Internships viii, 33, 34

Interview 19, 36, 40, 83, 141

Interview 92, 93, 94, 106, 107, 108, 109, 124, 125, 126, 127, 128, 129, 130, 131, 156, 157, 158, 189

L

Leisurewear 31

Liberal Arts vi, 46, 47, 53, 160

Lighting 22
LinkedIn 83

M

Makeup 78
Master's Degree 48, 49
Master's Degree 52
McKinsey & Company 5
Merchandising i, v, vii, 3, 4, 8, 9, 10, 12, 15, 28, 29, 36, 41, 42, 46, 49, 50, 56,
    64, 66, 76, 77, 82, 89, 99, 101, 102, 111, 112, 114, 115, 119, 132, 136, 137,
    141, 142, 145, 147, 148, 150, 151, 152, 161, 162, 166, 168

N

NCES ii, 47, 52
Networking 82
Nordstrom 30, 42, 43, 111, 114

P

Pandemic 5, 9, 12, 29, 30, 31, 59, 68, 69, 72, 73, 76
Pandemic viii, 5, 12, 75
Phishing 60
Piracy 60
Portfolio 34, 35, 49, 53, 66, 68, 97, 98, 99, 100, 101, 102, 103, 110, 111, 112,
    113, 114, 115, 116, 117, 118, 119, 120, 132, 133, 134, 135, 136, 137, 138,
    139, 140, 141, 142, 143, 144, 145, 146, 147, 148, 149, 150, 151, 152, 160,
    161, 162, 163, 165, 166, 167, 168, 169
Portfolio 92, 93, 94, 96, 98, 99, 100, 101, 102, 103, 106, 107, 108, 109, 110, 111,
    112, 113, 114, 115, 116, 117, 118, 119, 120, 124, 125, 126, 127, 128, 129,
    130, 131, 132, 133, 134, 135, 136, 137, 138, 139, 140, 141, 142, 143, 144,
    145, 146, 147, 148, 149, 150, 151, 152, 156, 157, 158, 160, 161, 162, 163,
    164, 165, 166, 167, 168, 169, 189
Producers 24
Proprietary 60

Q

Quarantine 5, 12, 29

R

Recycled 19, 22, 25
Rejection 71, 72
Restricted Early Action 69
Reusable 18
RFID 19, 20

S

SAT 66, 68, 69, 92, 93, 94, 106, 107, 108, 109, 113, 119, 124, 125, 126, 127, 128, 129, 130, 131, 141, 152, 156, 157, 158, 177, 178
Scholarships 43, 52, 57, 65, 66, 73, 96, 97, 98, 99, 100, 101, 102, 103, 110, 111, 112, 113, 114, 115, 116, 117, 118, 119, 120, 132, 133, 134, 135, 136, 137, 138, 139, 140, 141, 142, 143, 144, 145, 146, 147, 148, 149, 150, 151, 152, 160, 161, 162, 163, 164, 165, 166, 167, 168, 169
SlideRoom 96, 136, 189
Standardized test 68
Summer programs 34, 89, 139
Sustainable 18, 23, 25, 112

W

Waitlists 72
WeTransfer 40

www.ingramcontent.com/pod-product-compliance
Lightning Source LLC
Chambersburg PA
CBHW041935260326
41914CB00010B/1314